In,   ...-author,
with her sister, of the *Hand...   ...avellers* and is now
researching the relationship between English and Media Studies.

Many people take popular fiction as the model for their own writing.
Concentrating on girls' use of romance, Gemma Moss shows that they
are not mindlessly enslaved to the forms they reproduce, but are
actively deploying them to raise rich and complex questions about
social identity. *Un/Popular Fictions* examines the conflicting assumptions made about the role of texts in the social development of children,
suggests new strategies for classroom teaching, and offers new insights
into the ways in which cultural identities are negotiated.

Also in the Virago Education Series
In association with the University of London Institute of Education

Teaching Black Literature
Suzanne Scafe

Counting Girls Out
Girls and Mathematics Unit, Institute of Education
Compiled by Valerie Walkerdine

Un/Popular Fictions

Gemma Moss

VIRAGO

Published by VIRAGO PRESS Limited 1989
20–23 Mandela Street, Camden Town, London NW1 0HQ

Copyright © Gemma Moss 1989

A CIP catalogue for this book is
available from the British Library

Typeset in Great Britain by
Butler & Tanner Ltd, Frome and London

Printed by Cox & Wyman Ltd, Reading, Berkshire

Contents

Acknowledgements

I am indebted to the fourth-year English class whose work suggested the questions which led to this book. I would like to thank them all for being good company. For helping with the research, Angelique, Stephen, Joanna, Rachel, Corinna, Richard and Andy deserve special mention.

Special thanks to:

Angelique Miller for generously giving up her time to answer my many questions; Sarah Wolfender for sending me her soap opera, which I greatly enjoyed reading; Jane Miller for her encouragement and support throughout, and for always being on the end of a phone when I needed help and advice; David Buckingham for commenting on the manuscript at various stages and getting me to read some books I otherwise would have overlooked; Mary Brown, Bob Hall, Lucy Shepherd and Vanessa Coode for keeping me going during a long year in London (and more); Dena Attar for making some helpful comments on my work and above all being convinced that I could do it; and finally to Mike Chisholm, without whose long-suffering patience in listening to what I had to say, and disentangling my thoughts, a large part of this would never have got on to the page.

As for the thief who stole the small green rucksack containing my manuscript, all I would say now is 'Sock 'e'.

This book is for my parents, Rachel and Basil Moss.

1

A Feminist in the Classroom

When I first started teaching I was uncertain how to reconcile being a feminist with being a teacher. There were so many contradictions involved in trying to be both things at once. In the classroom I had more knowledge than my pupils, more responsibility for guiding their learning and setting boundaries to the activities they were involved in. By and large I would choose what they discussed, set the pace at which they worked and was probably alone in worrying about the outcome. My teaching practice notes and the sporadic diary I kept during my first year of teaching tell again and again of my anxieties about control and the establishment of my own authority as well as my fears that I was not doing a good enough job in teaching the individuals within my classes. What were they learning; was I stretching them enough; imposing my own ideas too much; closing down tentative lines of enquiry or leaving things so open-ended that lessons would dissolve in chaos, uncomfortable for all of us? All of this was in sharp contrast to the ways in which I was used to working as a feminist. In the women's movement no one individual expected to have absolute control over the agenda, each person was responsible to the group as a whole and the group was committed to working together, finding common ground and supporting each other's experience.

In the classroom power relations are inevitably unequal, and responsibility for what goes on rests ultimately with the teacher, not the taught, no matter how well-intentioned or liberal-minded the former may be. So it wasn't that one was a utopian dream to which I endlessly yearned to escape, faced with a nightmare present; rather that I couldn't put the two contexts together – they existed in parallel universes, separate spheres. How I worked as a feminist seemed to

have no direct bearing on my role as a teacher. It couldn't help me
out when it came to considering what to do next with a rowdy third
form. Nor did it inspire me to missionary work. I'd never conceived
of feminism as one person or one group of people having all the
answers and preaching their solution to others. The whole point of
being involved in the women's movement rather than in the organised
left was to search for other ways of sharing knowledge, identifying
problems and deciding what to do about them. The fundamental
starting point, be it a consciousness-raising or campaigning group,
was that each woman had as much to contribute as the others. If I
wasn't going to preach feminism, what else could I possibly do?
Somehow I had to find new ways of operating in a different context.

In my first year of teaching I ran a course on feminist issues as part
of the general studies programme for sixth-formers. The group which
opted for this subject included two girls and nine or ten boys. So
much for thinking this might provide the sort of feminist forum I was
familiar with. The two girls remained quiet and withdrawn, the boys
quickly took up positions for or against the equality of women, and I
was left running the course very much like any other academic subject:
taking along materials to read, statistics to discuss, worksheets to
tackle. The focal point for discussion became what I the teacher
presented, not the personal experience of the group themselves. This
was not what I had intended or wanted but it seemed unavoidable. I
didn't run the course again but moved on to other topics which seemed
easier to handle in this 'objective' fashion. I felt more comfortable
dealing with Third World issues in this way than controlling the
feminism I parcelled out for others to digest. If this was my difficulty
at the sixth-form level, where relationships between staff and students
were more relaxed, how could I even begin to hope for an equal
exchange of views lower down the school?

Of course, there were other issues to be taken up which didn't lead
straight into awkward questions about ways of organising, about my
authority and about the unequal power relations between myself and
my pupils. I started a girls' football club in the after-school slot where
staff were encouraged to run extracurricular activities. It was very
popular, particularly with first-year girls. My problem was that I knew
nothing whatsoever about football; neither did most of the girls,
though a few were already expert and playing for local teams. We

spent most of our time kicking the ball around the playground in a very haphazard fashion. I'm not sure now why we so rarely made it over to the football pitch for a proper game. We did challenge the first-year boys to a series of matches and won, or maybe we only drew. I can't remember. What I do recall is that as a way of bringing girls together and giving them some space and time it was fine, but they wanted more than that: someone to impart the skills I didn't have. Whether I was a committed feminist or not was not their concern. At the end of the year, with teachers' industrial action looming, the group folded.

Perhaps it was just as well: I'd run out of things I could teach and couldn't find anyone else to take on the commitment. Besides, some of the female PE staff were worrying that football detracted from the netball team they organised, and whereas the netball team had the possibility of competing against other schools, a football team hadn't. They were afraid of losing their best girls to football for no purpose. In setting up a girls' football team I had been inadvertently treading on other people's political toes. This, as I was beginning to discover, is inevitably part of the problem in working as a member of a large institution. Whatever you do as an individual sets up ripples and has repercussions. Moreover, as schools are organised hierarchically, what you do is also understood and interpreted according to the position of power you hold. Part of what I found myself having to work out was what I could say to whom, where and when, with what effect. It was not so much that I felt that I needed to be cautious − I generally realised that only after the event − as that I could see I was on the receiving end of other people's labelling. This was rather disturbing. I'd speak up in my normal fashion and find that at least as important as anything I'd said was the impression I'd created: 'Gosh, how daringly outspoken. What will the Head make of that?' 'How naively enthusiastic. She'll learn.' 'Well, that's a bit out of line, really, who does she think she is?' It was like talking into a ball of cotton wool; the ideas just got mopped up without comment. What got left over in full view was the way in which what had been said redefined or contributed to the complex network of power relationships being played out all around me. I had become part of some bizarre and complex game whose rules I didn't understand.

Schools as institutions are often slow-moving and cautious. Finding

even the time to raise the administrative issues I wanted considered was hard. I tried to get school registers discussed. These were kept alphabetically according to sex: girls first, boys second. No, they couldn't be reordered. End of discussion. The question of whether girls could be allowed to wear trousers in the summer term (they could during the autumn and winter, but not in the summer, when only skirts were allowed) went the same way. I wasn't sure where the proper forum for airing such matters was, where the real decisions got taken. Wherever it might have been, no one was telling me. I found myself constrained by holding too much power in relation to my pupils, too little in relation to the school as an institution.

It became harder to concentrate on what my role as a feminist teacher in the classroom might be. I became obsessed with how to keep my head above water in an institution whose ways of working seemed diametrically opposed to my own, a hierarchical structure which I found increasingly alienating. I was having to learn my place: at the bottom of an imposing pyramid. Far from rushing to the barricades to declare my position, I found myself looking for people simply to talk to. For a time I and some other women started a women's group together, but we were a very disparate lot, whose aims remained unclear. Were we operating as a mutual support group? But there was no consensus over what we might need support for. Were we trying to get policy issues discussed by the staff as a whole? A forlorn hope, this one, as none of us held positions inside the school power structure, so we had nowhere to take anything we came up with. Or were we trying to look at our own practice? But even here we didn't seem to know where to begin. Quite clearly we were not a consciousness-raising group, but I was unsure what else we might be or how else we could tackle things together.

When the teachers took industrial action I began to get involved in the union. Here at last was a context I could understand and felt at home in. People were only too grateful if you turned up with any ideas or proposals to put forward and the sort of status politics I was finding so confusing in school seemed not to apply. Ironically, having spent years castigating the organised left for their male-orientated ways of working I found myself escaping from school to the union with relief, despite the latter's formal ways of operating: the procedures, the votes, the points of order and the endless going over of the minutes of the

last meeting. I began to understand how I could be a feminist in this
context too, working alongside men in different ways. It wasn't so
much a question of tagging women's issues on to the business in
hand as recognising that my own feminism could provide a useful
perspective on a wide range of topics: the local authority's use of fixed-
term contracts, cover in schools, or how to organise union members
when we were out taking action. Above all, the union offered a place
in which to think through what I found so alienating and unpleasant
in the school structure. It also provided a forum in which to argue for
change and be listened to.

So far, in thinking back over my first years in teaching, I've been
mapping out my own political development. I had moved on from
seeing my feminism as being tied to working exclusively with other
women in particular ways to seeing it as adapting to meet a new
situation where I was working alongside (as well as against) men. In
the process, some of my confusions about working in school were
cleared up. Of course, the place didn't change, and power politics
remained the dominant feature, but at least I now understood that
and had a much clearer idea of what was happening to me there. Could
this change in perspective alter my own practice in the classroom and
help me to explore ways of working as a feminist outside a feminist
context? Having realised early on that I couldn't abolish the unequal
power relations in the classroom, what else was there I could do?

From the beginning I had always vetted with a critical eye the books
my English Department had in stock, and refused to use the most
misogynist ones. When using other books which inevitably slipped in
the occasional sexist comment I would interrupt the text to take issue
with it. What I did was largely determined by my own feelings. Some
books made me so angry I couldn't possibly have read them out loud.
I was also concerned that what we did read in class couldn't be used
by the boys as ammunition against the girls: 'Of course all girls don't
behave like that. It's ridiculous.' Censoring what we read or reacting
to it seemed relatively straightforward ways of tackling sexism in the
classroom. Whatever my difficulties in knowing what to do, here at
least I was clear that I could have an influence. For this reason also I
argued for the introduction of books showing girls taking active and
strong roles – *The Turbulent Term of Tyke Tyler*, for instance. Putting
forward alternative, positive images, I hoped, would undercut the

negative effects of the stereotypes we so often encountered. However, I became uneasy with what I was doing. Reading *Tyke Tyler* with a first-year class, I discovered that most of them had already read the book in primary school. The majority were sure it was about a boy: the ending had washed over them. I began to wonder. After all, in what sense was it about a girl? The lead character is in effect a boy, even if such a gender construction is largely dependent on the assumptions of the reader. Those assumptions would seem to be more compelling than the final revelation that Tyke is a girl.

I found myself further confused when faced with girl readers who avidly lapped up romances and wouldn't be drawn by any other stories: 'Find me a love story, Miss, a sad one.' So I did. Why shouldn't they read what they enjoyed? After all, I wasn't depriving the boys of their adventure stories and thrillers. But then, if anything, that was the sort of fiction I'd have preferred the girls to be reading – with female heroines, of course. In that case, did my feminism simply stand for a one-way traffic, girls into boys' areas? The girls could have my approval if they did what the boys did? I was clear that this wasn't what I was after, but I wasn't sure that I wanted girls to wallow in romances either. I didn't know what to make of what was going on. More than anything else, it was this sort of confusion which kept me from adopting a proselytising role in relation to my feminism. I just wasn't sure how what I had to say as a feminist matched up with the experience of the girls in my classes, or where they were coming from. Middle-class by background, from a family dominated by strong women (I also had no brothers), educated in a single-sex girls' grammar school, I found myself teaching in a mixed comprehensive in a largely working-class area where the girls seemed much more worldly-wise and capable than I had ever felt myself to be at their age. I felt out of my depth and profoundly uncertain how to judge what I saw. The girls who asked me for romances were rarely starry-eyed shrinking violets who seemed likely to be swept off their feet by the appearance of macho-man. They were more often than not tough, argumentative, assertive young women who were at least as likely to mouth off at the boys and tell them to get lost as they were to discuss eye make-up and jewellery or paint their fingernails at the back of my classroom.

I was struck by how much the girls seemed to know. Even in the first year they were quite clear that boys were a nuisance in class and that relations between the sexes often amounted to a barely disguised state of war. If some of the boys spent a lot of their time mocking girls, flexing their muscles and attempting to dominate the classroom space, girls spent a lot of their time fighting back. Often hostilities were quite open; at other times girls responded by ignoring the boys altogether: letting them talk big, act tough, whilst they quietly got on with their own lives around the edges of the classroom. At form time almost all friendship groups were single-sex. In classrooms that was how they chose to seat themselves. So much for trying to mix up the boys and girls. Weren't the girls already ahead of interventionist teachers here in coping with the problems boys posed them precisely by opting for single-sex groups? Girls didn't need to be told about male power; they were already dealing with it every day of their lives. Moreover, their understanding of what went on seemed infinitely more sophisticated than my own. For me at school boys had been a mysterious race apart whom I hadn't even bothered to consider until the teenage years propelled me into the possibilities of romantic encounters. Even then I'd considered them very much a side issue, something I had to know about but didn't need to get directly involved with. I was busy concentrating on my work and passing exams. I had led a cloistered existence. The girls I taught had far fewer illusions to lose.

I'm not trying to suggest that there weren't problems to be faced by the girls in my school, nor issues to be taken up. Quite clearly there were. Sexual harassment isn't something that happens only to adult women, nor is it committed only by adult men. Girls are often on the receiving end of a lot of aggressive behaviour, or on the contrary they may be overlooked and marginalised. Boys, on the other hand, are adept at getting more attention from their teachers in class, whilst subjects do often seem to revolve around their experience. But despite all this, the girls also struck me as survivors. If they weren't competing to disrupt lessons, that was because they were quietly choosing to get on with the business of learning, plodding through the tasks. I felt increasingly certain that my job was not so much to tell girls what to do as to support them in what they were already up to. I wasn't always clear what that was, but it seemed the right place to begin.

If I touched on certain themes I wouldn't have to say anything anyway; it would be the girls who made all the running. Housework was always a subject which would get the girls going: you had only to ask who did what at home and the hands would go up to voice complaints about unfair treatment: brothers got off scot-free whilst the girls had endlessly to help out. It was not a question of opening girls' eyes to the drudgery of domestic labour awaiting them in marriage so much as giving them the chance to air present grievances.

In working on this topic with a first-year class once, I got them to write a story about the day Mum went on strike and refused to do any more housework. I specifically asked them to resolve the crisis (which was to last several days) by the end of their stories. In almost all the girls' stories, Mum came off strike only after lengthy negotiations with the other members of the household and everyone promised to do more. The most popular ending in the boys' stories was where the son or husband presented Mum with a box of chocolates or a bunch of roses and she gave in to their expressions of appreciation. Nothing else changed. The girls' treatment of the stories suggested a realistic appraisal of the problems involved as well as an attempt to come up with fair solutions; the boys' seemed bound up in empty daydreams.

The more the girls' behaviour made sense, the stranger the boys' seemed. Just what were they up to? Why were so many of them spending so much of their time engaged in what I increasingly came to identify as peer power politics: mocking each other if they weren't mocking the girls, jostling with each other to establish their own status in the group, the class, the school? At form time I would watch what they did. Whilst the girls would sit in small groups of twos or threes – best friends, at least for the moment – the boys would sit round in much larger groups – sixes or sevens. These were much more public forums, with none of the quiet intimacy of the girls' conversations. With the noise level high, conversation raucous, they seemed to be spending most of their time trying to pick each other off by ganging up and making one of the group look foolish. In a moment it would be somebody else's turn to become the object of a never-ending cycle of derision, from which each member tried hard to escape by turning the spotlight back on someone else.

At the same time the groups themselves seemed stratified. There would be the tough nuts, each of whom fancied himself as one of the lads, practising physical stance as a means of impressing others and spending a lot of their time pushing each other off chairs or making loud farting noises and exploding into laughter. There were the brain-boxes, who distanced themselves from this sort of competition by being clever and discussing electronics or sport in serious tones, what they each knew being carefully weighed and measured by the rest of the group. And so on down, until you came to the group of wimps at the bottom of the heap, whom nobody wanted in their gang: too stupid, too weedy, with no social clout at all. Sometimes this last group would disperse themselves and tag along on the fringes of the other groups, seemingly grateful even to be the butt of others' jokes.

Weird! It wasn't that the girls didn't compete amongst themselves or give each other a hard time (best friends were always prone to busting up), but these things happened differently. They seemed to differentiate amongst themselves according to who was 'good' – at school work, at being responsible, or conversely at not caring for the rules – and this sort of evaluation seemed to depend on the judgement of others outside the group altogether, whether teachers or family, rather than being something you had to prove to your friends each time you got together. Moreover, the girls seemed much more tolerant of each other. Even the mousiest member of the class would have a best friend or at least be invited to sit with another pair. The one time there was a furious bust-up amongst the girls in my tutor group, with everybody sending a particular girl to Coventry, that girl was joined by just one other, who became her best friend.

As my understanding of what the girls and boys were up to became more complex, I found myself taking another look at the whole way in which English teachers talked about issues of gender. The matter was not a high-priority one in my own department, and whereas I do remember us endlessly discussing mixed-ability teaching and pro-grammes of work for first to fifth years I don't recall us starting a department meeting with gender as the main topic. I was too uncertain of my own views to have suggested this. Maybe others were too. Nevertheless, the matter would often be raised tangentially. In relation to book buying I remember everybody falling eagerly upon *Nobody's Family is going to Change* as a wonderful example of a non-racist, non-sexist text which was also a good read, and there was a general interest in buying more books with a girl as the central character: *The Friends*, *The Great Gilly Hopkins*, for example. These seemed straightforward matters.

More contentious was the way in which considerations of gender surfaced in relation to marking. Many colleagues would bemoan the predominance of the romance form in girls' writing. Such work was often dismissed as uninteresting drivel, and stigmatised as clichéd and stereotyped. The attitude seemed to be that girls were wasting their time writing this sort of stuff and should be getting on with something more serious. Sometimes, when moderating exam essays, I would find romances which seemed to have been marked down below the grade I felt they justified on the grounds of content rather than of technical competence or of use of language. This interested me because only the romance as a form seemed to attract this sort of adverse reaction. The stuff I found particularly tedious – boys' science-fiction epics filled with strangely named computer parts, or endless car chases, or complicated hijacks – seemed to escape the watchful marker's eye and pass unchallenged. Just as I'd found myself unable to take a hard-and-fast line in relation to girls reading romances, so too I felt ambivalent about their use of the form in their writing. Were we just applying double standards here by assuming that the romance was more dangerous to girls than the thriller was to boys? Is the romance malicious ideology on the move, warping girls' desires, bounding their horizons with thoughts of love and marriage? If it was, then how did that judgement fit with my sense of the girls in my classes as strong and resourceful individuals who maybe had no lasting answers to the problems boys caused them but were in no doubt that such problems existed? Once you made the assumption that the romance was inherently reactionary and against the girls' own best interests there seemed no way of avoiding being contemptuous of the writers or at best pitying them for having been so easily deceived.

I became increasingly interested in untying this particular knot. By taking a pro-woman line, couldn't I come up with some alternative explanation of what was going on when girls used the romance form, which might validate their actions rather than casting them only as hapless victims of a sexist society? So many of the other assumptions I had brought to the classroom about the way things would be for the girls had already turned out to be wrong, didn't this whole area need closer examination?

These are the questions which, more than any others, have stayed with me and out of which the rest of this book has grown. In getting to an answer I have found myself moving outside the perimeters of what I would once have identified as feminist questions and examining questions about English teaching as a whole. In particular I have found myself exploring the range of attitudes that English teachers bring to their marking of children's work. From looking at the sorts of comments teachers make when they mark, I have moved to considering how teachers conceptualise the act of writing itself. What do we imagine is going on when children pick up a pen and write? Because my interest in this whole topic arose from queries about the way the romance form is used in girls' writing, I have also been concerned to re-examine the supposed relationship between the texts children read and those they write. What influence do texts, particularly popular fiction texts, exert on their readers? At the same time I have wanted to keep in mind the way in which considerations of gender insist on creeping into the issues. Too much of the talk about writing and reading in education treats children as if they were one homogeneous entity and forgets that they are also girls and boys.

The central focus for my work has been three pieces of writing produced by pupils in one of my fourth-year English groups. Two of these, written by girls, are romances; the other, written by a boy, is an adventure story. Rereading these stories, taking them apart and seeing how they worked, provided the original starting point for this enquiry. Those rereadings are to be found in Chapters 4 and 5. They are framed by my more general enquiries into the nature of writing, and the possibilities for dealing with gender in the classroom in new ways.

2

Style and Authenticity: Teachers Reading Children's Writing

I want to begin this chapter by taking a brief look at the way in which a particular piece of writing was marked. My interest here is in the range of comments made and what those comments suggest about the sorts of assumptions that English teachers bring to their marking.

The narrative from which the extracts below were taken was written by a girl in a second-year class. It is an extended piece of writing which was to fill the whole of one exercise book and continue halfway into another. The pupil had been asked to write a soap opera. The lesson in which the assignment was given was English, and the written instructions which preceded the piece itself in the child's book were as follows:

A few hints on how to write a soap opera.

1. Choose a set that you know something about.
2. End each episode with suspense.
3. Plan your sub-plots.

Sarah, the girl who wrote the piece, called it *What a life* and chose as her setting a medical school at Cambridge University. She listed ten characters before she started writing, telling the reader a little about each one, the following being a typical entry:

Joe Lee She has just passed her A levels, every grade was an A so she sent off for Cambridge and she has got in. She has dark hair and brown eyes.

The story begins with the new students arriving in Cambridge. It continues following their fortunes as they train. The main interest is in the evolving relationships between Joe Lee and an older student,

Charles, and between another of the first-year students, Andrew, and his teacher, Ms Rabbit. The sub-plot is provided by an account of what happens to Nicholas and his teacher, Mr Murffy, when the latter spends most of his time plying them both with drink. The villain of the piece is the secretary, Alice Edgley, who spends all her time trying to get everyone else into trouble. Because the story is so long I haven't quoted it in full, but the following extracts give a good idea of what it is like. The first extract comes from the beginning of the story and starts when the new students are being allocated their teachers:

'Sarah Knight your teacher will be Miss Bragg in room 12. Nicholas your teacher will be Mr Murffy and he will be in room 39. Andrew Langton your teacher will be Ms Rabbit and she will be in room 49. Now is that everybody. Would you like to go to the rooms now.'

'Sir,' said a young lady, 'You have forgotten me' she said

'No you must be Anna, I am going to be your teacher'

'Oh yes I see.'

Everybody had found their room except Johnathan, he was totally lost, then a young student passed him. 'excuse me but are you looking for something' she said 'Yes I'm looking for room 19' he said. 'Oh its this way' she showed him the way to the room. He knocked on the door a voice from inside said 'do come in' Johnathan went in the room.

'Ah you must be Johnathan please take a seat, now why did you want to be a doctor?' She didn't let him get a word in, she talked him to death.

Nicholas had found Mr Murffy quite easily and they were in this small room having a good laugh, then Mr Murffy brought out a bottle of gin and poured out two glasses, and they started to drink it. 'Have some more Nick, drink up. Oh yes call me Pat'. It wasn't long before they were both drunk. They were singing 'The hills are alive' all out of tune.

'Mr Murffy is that you again?'

(What will happen, will they get thrown out for boing drunk, or will they try and act sober. Who is calling them find out in chapter 3)

Chapter three

There was a lot of laughter. 'Will you shut up Mr Murffy you do this every year, you always get drunk.'

'Oh I am sorry Ms Cathcock, but I'm not drunk'

'Not drunk you could have fooled me'

She ran round the corner and came back with a large bucket of water. She walked up to them and poured it all over their heads.

'Good god woman what have you done, a new clean suit this is, and you've ruined it!'

'Well it serves you right Mr Murffy, now go and get dried up'

The both of them were still drunk so they didn't care. They both walked out of the building for some reason and fell in the duck pond.

People were in rooms learning things and Nicholas and Mr Murffy are drunk in the duck pond.

'Mr Murffy I warned you'

'Oh its you again is it, can't you see I'm doing something' He said.

'Get out you stupid man, and act like a grown up!'

'Oh do shut up Mrs Cathcock'

'Ms Cathcock, if you please, you're acting like a four year old.'

'Oh shut up you old bag.' He said, and he got out and pulled her in the pond.

She was screaming for help and it was only three foot deep.

While all this was happening Andrew Longton was at the other side of the building with Ms Rabbit, they were both being very serious, and Andrew was really pleased with what teacher he had. He just couldn't keep his eyes off her.

The second extract comes from the middle of the story when Ms Shar Rabbit has invited her student, Andrew, back to her house for a meal.

Andrew and Shar were sitting down eating bacon and egg.

'Oh Shar that was lovely.'

'Oh do you think so?'

'Yes, Um I think I had better be going'

'Oh, do you?'

'Yes I've got some work to catch up on'

He went over and picked up his bike.

'Oh no both tyres have got a puncture'

'Oh dear how are you going to get home'

'I suppose I'll walk'

'Don't be silly you live over five miles away'

'I know'

'Look you can stay here the night on the sofa'

'Oh could I that would be lovely'

'Yes, I'll just make some more coffee'

'Oh'

He sat down on the sofa feeling very happy.

'Now make your self at home and drink your coffee' said Shar

Then they both sat back in the sofa, then Andrew put his arm round Shar.

'Oh Andrew'

'Oh Shar'

and they fell into each others arms and started kissing, and they got up and went into the bedroom

The action in the third extract takes place towards the end of the story when Alice Edgley has overheard Ms Shar Rabbit telling Andrew that he is the father of the child she is expecting. Alice loses no time in passing the news on to everybody else. Consequently, when Shar realises what is going on, she decides to tackle Alice.

Now everybody knew about Shar being pregnant, but Shar didn't want anybody to know, but Alice had to start trouble. Shar was looking for Alice, then she saw her.

'Alice come here!'

'Pardon?'

'Get your backside over here now.'

'What's the matter?'

'You know what's the matter'

'No I don't'

'Listening to people's private conversations, that's what!'

'Oh that!'

'Well I think you have got some explaining to do'

'Me, you're the one who's got some explaining to do' said Alice

'Why me?'

'You and Andrew doing you know what'

'Well, Alice, that's my business isn't it'

'Maybe it is, but I think you have got a cheek'

'Me, I don't listen to people's private conversations, and then tell everybody them'

'Well, Ms Rabbit, I hope you get the sack for being so disgusting.'

'Hu, the reason why you have never had children was because nobody liked you'

'Right you old bag, you've asked for it'

And she hit Shar across the face.

'Hu you ugly prat!' said Shar and she hit her back.

They were in a big room just on their own and they were just about to beat each other up until Andrew came in.

'Alice get off Shar'

'Oh daddy's come has he' said Alice

'Shut up before I break your face.'

'Shar! you wouldn't dare, just in case you lost your little baby.'

'Shut up Alice, I would' said Andrew.

Then Mike burst in the room, 'Oh Alice up to my office now,' and she sauntered off down the corridor.

'Are you OK Shar?' said Mike.

'Yes I'm fine.'

'Look I'll see you two later. I've got to sort out Alice.'

He went out, and walked down the coridoor and went into his office and slammed the door.

'Right Alice you were warned not to start trouble. I am going to report you'

'Oh Mike, don't'

'I am going to report you now go away', and she went off.

These extracts are typical of the story as a whole. There is a rapid sequence of events and a considerable reliance on dialogue both to keep the action moving and to let the reader know what individual characters are thinking and feeling or planning to do. The moments which the author chooses to concentrate on are moments of high drama and excitement or events which can be written about with humour; not the ordinary, routine and everyday. The fast pace, the complexity of the plots and sub-plots and the emphasis on conflict between characters are all familiar features of soap operas. Yet it is not set out as a play script, and any sense of what camera shots might be involved has to be inferred from the prose narration rather than being explicitly stated. So whilst the author borrowed certain aspects of the way soap operas function to use in her story, there is no sense that she is writing with the techniques of television production in mind.

Perhaps this is not surprising, given that this piece of work has been produced as an English rather than a Media Studies assignment. Part of the aim of Media Studies as a subject is to take a careful look at the way particular artefacts are structured and produced, and such an analysis would certainly precede any practical work set for students. English is often vaguer about the connection between anything that has been read before a student writes and the latter's work. Where links are made, the invitation is usually to borrow settings and characters. Quite what the students will do with these is open to their own interpretation, so what goes on in any one story is seen to be very much the child's own business once the title has been established as a trigger for their response.

The directions given for writing this soap opera seem to operate like this. There is nothing about them to indicate that the author should be considering her work as anything other than the same sort of writing task routinely undertaken in English lessons: a story. Neither the directions nor the writing itself suggest that any time has been spent in lessons watching soap operas and identifying how they work so that that exact knowledge can be translated into the writing. The directions' stress on the need for careful planning of sub-plots and suspense at the end of each episode could just as well be requirements for writing a novel.

If the invitation to write in English lessons looks comparatively open-ended, what happens when pupils' work is marked? It is hard to see how teachers could evaluate the work they receive unless they already have a set of criteria for success or failure, even if these criteria aren't explicitly stated. Bearing this in mind I want to turn now to the comments made on Sarah's soap opera by her teacher. Almost two-thirds of them were to do with spelling and punctuation, such as 'Use words not numbers' and 'Your main mistake is accuracy of punctuation: you must have *some* mark of punctuation *before you close your speech marks*.' As one might expect, the piece acts most importantly as a way of assessing the mechanical skills of writing. Of the remaining comments some were straightforwardly evaluative, for example 'A good story line', and seemed designed to encourage the writer. The rest were as follows:

> I would have liked the description of the building here
> Who is talking now? Are you in the story now?
> I think they would be called 'tutors' rather than 'teachers'
> I think the sort of people who go to Cambridge do often get drunk and wild, but they are not usually rude to women without a good reason.
> Interesting developments. Don't have too much conversation, have some more description
> That's very quick. It would have been nicer to have a bit of nice romantic description here ('There were stars in her eyes' type of thing)
> *A lot of hard work.* A good story line with a lot of complications! I think

if you had decided on Cambridge as your setting, you could have tried to make the people sound *posher*. I would have liked more description of people and places.

This sounds more like East Enders than posh would-be doctors in Cambridge.

I like your 'Soap' style questions at the end of each chapter! Great! I think the violence is a bit too much though. I think people often manage to sail through difficult situations without quite so many cheap insults and aggression, especially if they fancy themselves to be well educated.

I am most impressed by how much work you've produced, but I *hope* doctors, or even students, are better mannered people in their private lives.

The hidden agenda here seems to be first, that characters and events should be realistically portrayed. Much of the teacher's argument with the pupil's work is that doctors and medical students would not really behave like this. This stress on realism is underlined by the fact that the first of the teacher's directions for writing a soap opera was to 'choose a set that you know something about'. Second, that it is important to employ one particular stylistic feature associated with another kind of writing: description. The child's work is found wanting because there is not enough 'description of people and places'. And finally, that writing is not without moral consequences. In this respect the teacher is concerned to challenge moments at which violence or casual sex seem to be handled frivolously.

This is a rather odd mixture of comments. They look particularly strange when set against the invitation to write a soap opera. Indeed, the teacher seems to have had most difficulty in responding to those incidents in the story which are most like their soap-opera equivalents. The comment about being rude to women appears alongside the incident where Ms Cathcock is thrown in the duck pond, the comments about 'EastEnders' and too much violence occur in the chapter where Shar confronts Alice and refer to this incident, whilst the comment on romantic description is made at the point where Andrew and Shar, who have just started kissing each other on the sofa at Shar's house, get up and make straight for the bedroom. There seems to be a considerable mismatch between what the teacher expected and what the child wrote in response to a very general brief. For the pupil the soap opera has suggested an episodic structure with plenty of suspense and melodramatic action. For the teacher it seems to have functioned more as a stimulus for an extended piece of writing, with a fairly disparate set of requirements to be met beyond that. It is to the hidden requirements for writing that underpin much of the work that goes on in English that I now want to turn. I have two questions: What are the assumptions about the nature of good writing which inform the sorts of comments teachers make when marking and, conversely, govern the kinds of work children themselves produce?

It is still common practice for English Departments to set down a year-by-year syllabus for pupils. One example in my possession outlines the following under the heading 'Personal Writing for the First–Third Years':

Year 1: Emphasis on self, surroundings, friends and relatives, myth and legend, adventure. Thematic work. Some simple poem writing, avoiding rigid rhyme.

Year 2: Emphasis on feelings, memories, reactions, impressions, magic and mystery. Opportunity for longer prose pieces to be written. Thematic work.

Year 3: Techniques in writing the formal 'set essay'. Note-making, valid approaches, style, topics such as aspects of fashion and the youth culture, old age, the future, realistic adventure. Collective writing of radio plays. Thematic work. Class anthology of poetry and prose, newspaper or magazine.

and alongside under the heading 'Formal Writing':

Year 1: Factual accounts of own interests, hobbies, sports and games. Personal letters describing events and places. Simple written comprehension. How to use a dictionary.

Year 2: Interpreting and giving instructions. Technical accounts of processes and objects. Written comprehension. The formal rules of letter writing. Simple newspaper style reports.

Year 3: Summary of passages from text books, novels, newspapers etc. Note taking from taped lectures. Writing factual reports based on research into reference books. Comprehension work.

Whilst not beginning by restricting the child entirely to personal writing this is, nevertheless, where the emphasis falls in the first years. The more formal and distanced styles of writing are not dealt with until later. Such practice is undoubtedly motivated by a reading of James Britton and relies on his categorisation of language into expressive, transactional and poetic; and with him it assumes that children start with the expressive:

> A young child's speech will be expressive for the very reason that in his egocentrism he finds it difficult or impossible to escape from his own point of view, to take into account his 'listeners' – or indeed to suppose that 'things as they are' could differ from 'things as he sees them'. (Britton, James, 1970, p. 169)

> It is when the demand is made for participant language that *any reader* can follow, or to spectator role language to satisfy an *unknown reader* that the pressure is on for a move from expressive writing to transactional and poetic writing respectively.... Children will not be able to comply fully with these demands at once. (ibid., p. 174)

Such a developmental view of writing – from the expressive to the poetic and transactional – is the recurrent theme in *Writing and Learning Across the Curriculum 11–16* (Martin, Nancy, *et al.*, 1976), where the authors use their understanding that 'expressive writing ... is the seed bed from which more specialised and differentiated kinds of writing can grow' (p. 26) to develop a critique of the sort of learning and writing on offer across the secondary-school curriculum:

> What is worrying is that in much school writing the pupil is expected to exclude expressive features and to present his work in an unexpressive transactional mode. The demand for impersonal, unexpressive writing can actively inhibit learning because it isolates what is to be learned from the vital learning process – that of making links between what is already known and new information. (p. 26)

In mounting this critique they offer a challenge to the traditional notions of how subjects such as humanities and science are best taught and create the space in which to argue that talk and first-hand experience are essential tools for learning.

In relation to English teaching, however, Britton's categories also dovetail quite neatly with existing practice. Take my own English Department, for example. The range of questions on our CSE essay papers reflected the tripartite division of language into expressive, transactional and poetic, although they were rarely discussed in those

terms. There would be the title calling for an autobiographical piece
of writing:

> *Introducing my family.*
> Choose one or two members of your family to write about. Think carefully.
> What sort of people are they? How do you get on with them? Try to
> remember a particular incident which shows them at their worst, and an
> occasion which shows them at their best. Now write about them in detail.

The title asking for the discursive essay:

> *In trouble with the Law.*
> Write about the following:
>
> a) Why do young people turn to crime?
> b) What is the best way to stop people committing crime?

or

> 'A man's place is in the home, cooking and bringing up the children; a
> woman's place is to go out to work to support her family.'
> Discuss this view as fully as you can.

And those titles asking the writer for 'creative writing':

> Locked in a museum; The accident; The station at midnight.

In deciding how to mark the writing produced in answer to these sorts
of titles it is easy enough to give credit for autobiographical writing
which speaks personally of the writer and to weigh that against mechanical difficulties; in the discursive essay to search for signs that the
writer is aware of more than one argument and can put forward their
own point of view coherently and persuasively. But with creative
writing it is harder to know exactly what the teacher is looking for.
The titles above in this latter category could give rise to all sorts of
different writing: an atmospheric piece of description in which nothing
much happens, but attention to small details creates a sense of mood
and place; a piece of social realism in which the emphasis is on
character and setting, where conflict and feelings will be explored; or
a piece of formula writing – a ghost story, a thriller or a romance –
where events are melodramatic and the action is fast and furious.

It is creative writing that I want to concentrate on here. So far I
have been working on the assumption that Britton's categories of

expressive, transactional and poetic are in some sense interchangeable with autobiographical, discursive and creative, as far as the teacher is concerned. Does the category poetic, with all that it implies, help the teacher to assess creative writing?

Britton defines poetic use of language as 'more of a performance, more of a construction, a verbal object' (Britton, James, 1970, p. 170) and again: 'A reader is asked to respond to a particular verbal construct which remains quite distinct from any other verbal construct anybody else might offer' (ibid., p. 175). Nancy Martin *et al.* say of poetic writing:

> It leaves us free to attend to its formal features – which are more implicit than explicit – the pattern of events in a narrative, the configuration of an idea, above all the pattern of feelings evoked. (1976, p. 25)

These quotations are reminiscent of the Russian Formalists who, in their attempt to differentiate between literary language and the ordinary language of speech, saw the former as 'making strange', drawing attention to itself. For the Formalists, 'words in poetry have the status not simply of vehicles for thoughts but of objects in their own right, autonomous, concrete entities.' Thus literary works 'at the same time that they speak the language of reference, also emit a kind of lateral message about their own process of formation' (Hawkes, T. E., 1977, pp. 63, 67).

I am not suggesting that Britton and Martin have necessarily borrowed from Formalism to define the poetic; what I would suggest is that the similarity of approach is more probably a result of taking as the object of study the same thing – good literature – for it is surely here that the poetic finds its purest expression. So how useful is such a definition, conceived through attention to professional literary writing, when applied to children's work? Part of the problem seems to lie not so much with the conception of 'poetic', as expounded by Britton, but with the way it is used and understood by teachers. For in practice the category 'poetic', in focusing attention on language and form, most neatly dovetails with the English teacher's long-standing preoccupation with style: the means to improving children's writing.

Taken at its loosest style means the way things are written about, the focus here varying from a concern for the text as a whole through lexical choice to sentence construction. The O level examination boards, in their annual reports on the English Language papers, comment on all these aspects of the essays submitted for assessment as well as commenting on spelling, handwriting and punctuation:

> It is always tempting to write at length; there were several compositions over a thousand words long, but they might have made more impact had they been shorter and more tightly structured. (University of London, 1978, p. 121)

> Many alleged 'compositions' were collections of bald statements sometimes in single sentence 'paragraphs', with all the grace and charm of a cookery recipe. Others stuttered along without regard to form or sequence, lacking any development, extension or illustration of ideas. (AEB, 1980, p. 11)

Often examiners spend a considerable amount of time commenting on lexical choice:

> Inappropriate expressions are still in evidence and tend to reflect current television jargon, or what an examiner castigated as 'disc-jockey jabber'. (AEB, 1981, p. 25)

The contrast drawn is between colloquial phrases and what are seen as the demands of written English:

> Many of [the candidates] were happy to chat on colloquially in much the same language as they would use to their school mates, and seemed unaware of the need to write formally. (AEB, 1980, p. 12)

Whatever the particular feature of the work being discussed, the word which crops up more frequently than any other is 'appropriate'. That is to say, examiners look for the sort of expression which they consider to be appropriate to the form, the subject matter and the context, the latter being one where the examiners will do the reading (hence the complaint about the presence of language used with 'school mates' above).

> The most successful compositions tend to be those in which ... the style used is appropriate to the topic chosen so that a suitable tone is established and sustained, frequently through the control of sentence structure and the range of vocabulary employed. (University of London, 1978, p. 121)

Candidates' work is rewarded if the 'appropriate' style has a 'good' effect on the reader:

The assessment was primarily based on the compositions' *positive* qualities, such as the unity of overall impression, the treatment of material which engages a reader's attention and establishes both a point of view and a context, and the clarity, coherence and appropriateness of style. (University of London, 1984, p. 206)

The way a piece is written – its style – therefore plays a very important part in the whole process of assessment and evaluation at public examination. Despite the trenchant way in which the examiners express their views in the extracts above, there is considerable agreement amongst teachers as to just what constitutes a good piece of work. Indeed, the consensus is such that almost all examination boards use impression marking to evaluate written work. Yet although we all seem to know what we mean when we talk about a well-written story, essay or composition, actually defining what we mean in the abstract rather than in the context of a particular piece of writing seems hard. This difficulty shows up in the sort of advice we give to pupils when we are trying to help improve their work. Take the following as an example. It comes from a book called *Exploring Language with Children*:

1. Which of my sentences say what I want to say the 'best' way they can? Are there some which don't really say anything at all? Are there places where I've expected a reader to jump wider gaps in action than anyone can safely jump? Is there a way I can arrange my sentence to make it more interesting (funny, engaging, descriptive, unexpected, shorter, longer, tantalizing)?

2. Are there words in my story which need to be made stronger? For example, *nice*, that pale modern-day ancestor of the vigorous Middle English adjective meaning wanton, is now so anaemic it can seldom holds its own in a sentence. Children can be helped to see that many words need to be weeded out of their vocabulary because they are today too feeble to be effective. (Stewig, J., 1974, p. 204)

Almost all the terms used to guide the writers' assessment of what they've written (presumably with a view to redrafting and thereby gaining a better grade) are relative: best, wider, more interesting, stronger, too feeble. What is being compared to what here? The author does not make it clear. It's almost as if we assume that children – just like us – will automatically be able to recognise the best style, the most appropriate thing to say, even if we can none of us define exactly what that is. Writing about how one student's comments on another's work led to the revision and subsequent improvement of that piece, Brian Johnston says of the commenting student: 'It is important to emphasize that Chris received no lengthy training before making this response. He demonstrated that this detailed responsiveness was available, simply waiting to be tapped' (Johnston, Brian, 1987). Well, I would like to know more than that. Where does the knowledge that allows us to ask 'What's missing at this part of the text?' or to state 'I need to know more here' come from?

Britton's definition of the poetic seems to have arisen from the consideration of literary texts. Can the same be said of the criteria we apply when marking children's work, and if so exactly what does this lead us to look for? Britton's definition of the poetic as quoted above seems rather ambitious when considering children's actual writing, no matter how good. If asked to define the sort of writing which gets less than the top marks – leaving aside technical features such as spelling, punctuation and so forth – the sort of list that any teacher might produce would probably look something like this:

Plots are often too complex and the length within which the child is working leaves insufficient space to resolve the action satisfactorily. Endings are weak.

The action dominates to the point where it becomes a series of loosely connected episodes which fail to cohere into a unified text, and in cramming the text with events the child dispenses with detail.

There is little room for character development.

Dialogue lies woodenly on the page.

Events themselves are far-fetched and the author makes little attempt to engage the reader's interest.

The detail that is included seems haphazard, and may degenerate into a simple listing of parts.

Adjectives are few and far between, or leap out awkwardly from the page, self-consciously drawing attention to the disjuncture between themselves and the rest of the text.

There are abrupt shifts in tone. A sentence which begins in a literary register suddenly switches to colloquialisms.

The whole thing bores the exasperated teacher ploughing through pages of the stuff. There's no web of feeling to be entered into and shared.

Plot control, atmosphere, sense of character and place, with a stress on the need for the text to be viewed as a coherent whole – these are notions transplanted from literary criticism. The faults we identify in a text, therefore, are established, by and large, with reference to other forms of literature and other readings teachers have made. What is particularly ironic about this is that in producing their 'bad' writing, children are almost certain to be leaning just as extensively as the teacher on other texts. Just as the teacher, in assessing such writing, may be looking for the presence of certain features assumed to be shared with other literary texts, so the child, in the actual process of writing, may be seeking first and foremost to reproduce features of other texts. The trouble is that they almost certainly won't be the same ones.

The notion of what constitutes a good story for teachers is established for them by their acquaintance with 'good' literature – that is, literature which is accepted by academic institutions as being worthy of study. The method of critical study may well induce the reader to privilege certain features of the text: its ability to move the reader powerfully, opening up other doors of experience, ennobling the reader, if you're a Leavisite; its ambivalence and ambiguity, if you're a New Critic; its sense of underlying structure if you're a Structuralist; its location within the social world if you're a Marxist. By and large all these approaches have assumed until recently that any text is a unified coherent whole and that it is the reader's duty, no matter how difficult the task might seem at first glance, to establish how the disparate parts fit together. In recent years, of course, this underlying assumption has been the focus of much critical attack, most notably at the hands of the Post-Structuralists, amongst whom Derrida and Barthes are probably the best known. But most teachers will have passed through English Departments in universities long before such theory began to have any impact on the British scene. Moreover, it is assumed that what is sought in texts can be found only in some texts, the canon of good literature. Most popular literature is excluded from the area of serious study – or if it is admitted, then it is to examine it as a reservoir of stereotyped images and untruths, palming itself off as the real thing on an unsuspecting and uncritical audience: the average reader. What is to be studied is how such second-rate stuff manages to perpetrate such deceit, when the critical reader can instantly see through it.

Yet when children undertake creative writing and choose to base their work on something other than their own experience it is precisely this other sort of literature – popular fiction – which they work from. Drawing from books, television or film, they reproduce the genres of the romance, the thriller, the ghost story, or science fiction. Sue May has shown, in 'Story in its writeful place' (in Miller, Jane (ed.), 1984, pp. 27–42), how in so doing they concentrate on and isolate some of the formal features of the work. But they are drawing on precisely that body of literature which meets with teacherly disapproval: the sorts of books which are not used as class readers, the sorts of books whose presence in the school library may be tolerated but not encouraged. And they get little credit for it. Examination board reports are spattered with the following sorts of disparaging comments:

> The stories ... varied from those with a spark of inventiveness to those that were stereotyped and trivial. If the candidates had visualised the scene in the isolated village, they would have been less prone to fantastic imaginative flights, less disposed to introduce bizarre incidents and melodramatic situations. (AEB, 1961, p. 104)

> The best candidates were able to sustain the initial situations that they established, whereas weaker candidates settled for accounts of robberies with confused and over-ingenious plots. (University of London, 1984, p. 208)

> Poorer candidates resorted rapidly to armed robberies which they were fortunate to witness and to foil. (ibid.)

Indeed, it is precisely those stylistic features of the children's writing which most nearly approximate to the models of popular fiction that are the most roundly condemned: flat characterisation, sparse use of detail, complex plots, with the stress on action.

Frank Whitehead, in *The Disappearing Dais*, criticises a passage from one of the Biggles books in terms which echo only too clearly the remarks of the examiners above:

> interest and tensions are maintained almost entirely by an unrelenting accumulation of incident; there is no dwelling on any single item in the sequence, and little attempt at any genuinely realised immediacy of presentation.... Technical terms are used freely but unspecifically, their function being more to impart atmosphere than to define any particular happening.... This exclusive reliance on fast-moving external action naturally leaves no room for any development of the emotional quality of the situation described. As far as human motives, thoughts and sensations are concerned, the writer is content to ring the changes upon a singularly limited repertoire of conventional stereotypes. (Whitehead, Frank, 1966, pp. 51–2)

When this sort of formula writing is not subjected to this kind of attack, it is virtually ignored. Children's writing is attracting a considerable amount of professional interest in education circles these days, particularly amongst English teachers, yet of the many books on the subject none makes more than passing reference to writing which draws on popular fiction. Instead, current debate concerns itself predominantly with personal writing drawn from the children's own experience; realist imaginative texts which evoke a context the authors are assumed to know something about, even if the events themselves aren't believed to have actually happened; and the argumentative or factual essay, where an opinion is being put forward or a body of information assembled.

I am as intrigued by the silence on the subject of formula writing as I am by the vehemence of the condemnation, not least because in my own experience of marking CSE examination scripts it is precisely this sort of writing that predominates. When it came to dividing up the fourth- and fifth-year examination essays according to title for distribution to markers, it was always the title that lent itself most readily to a formula-fiction response that would have attracted by far the largest number of candidates. Why, then, do we have so little to say about it? Part of the trouble seems to be that writing which draws on popular fiction for its subject matter, form or expression is not seen to display the qualities teachers most value in writing, even when it is stylistically competent and technically accurate, the plot coherent and the text capable of being read as a unitary whole. A further look at the examiners' reports shows that creative writing is most valued if it has originality, gives the impression that the writer is speaking from the heart, or engages the reader with questions of importance:

> A common failing among candidates might best be summed up as under
> confidence. Very few seemed to see the value of writing from their own
> experience with precision and honesty. Many resorted to a kind of mimicry
> which they believed would impress the examiner, and appeared to value
> a superficial slickness more than the ability to say something which they
> genuinely felt or thought. (AEB, 1981, p. 30)

To gain approval, candidates' writing should not be reproducing stock
characters, stock responses:

> The essays rarely showed any kind of actual observation and an awareness
> of the trees or people or whatever. Is no one taught to use eyes and ears
> now? Do today's young people really have such a barren intellectual
> landscape? Yet amid much cliché of situations and emotion, with the
> pathetic fallacy in its most lurid forms, every now and then a piece
> of honest, clear-sighted writing did emerge, instinct with feeling and
> observation, that lifted the examiner's heart and brought a lump to the
> throat. (SUJB, 1986, p. 44)

Above all it should bear the hallmark of individuality. A writer who
attempts the latter will be forgiven stylistic flaws:

> Although there was much delightfully fresh writing, many of the essays
> were dull and predictable. Examiners respond readily to the lively, original
> treatment of the subjects. The girl who would like a different mink for
> each day of the week and the boy who said that life in a large family was
> hell probably gained extra marks for 'swimming against the tide'. (SUJB,
> 1967, p. 5)

'Precision', 'honesty', the 'genuinely felt', 'clear-sighted', 'instinct
with feeling and observation', 'original' – all these qualities sought in
the text are also somehow seen to be the property of the writers
themselves. The assumption is that to attain this quality of work
writers only have to pay closer attention to the way things are, develop
sensitive insight into their own feelings, attune the sensitivity of their
own response, concentrate on the quality of their own imagination.

Dixon and Stratta, in an article on developing personal narrative,
make the following comments when explaining why they find a particular piece of a child's story 'disappointing':

> The writer seems to have lost an imaginative grip on the story; the

narrator's position fizzles out, and the events are summary – no longer offered from a felt, personal point of view. (This imaginative insecurity had already peeped through with an orchard being raided at Easter, and an eleven foot wall being scaled 'easily' by the narrator!) (Dixon, John and Stratta, Leslie, 'Achievements in Writing at 16 + ')

The fact that what might otherwise be called a mistake – 'an orchard being raided at Easter' – is here treated as a sign of 'imaginative insecurity' is interesting. I would suggest that Dixon and Stratta are able to say this because of their understanding of what being a writer means, and this understanding draws very much on what one might characterise as a Romantic view of poets and authors: that truly creative artists qualify for such a title because of the quality of their vision, a quality which finds its simple reflection in their work. To be an artist you need nothing more than refined sensibilities. If you take this view of writers – that they 'have a strong sense of the individual quality of each moment of experience' – then it is no wonder that so much attention focuses on personal writing, for it follows that it is precisely by paying close attention to your own experience that great writing emerges. For from the Romantic perspective the original is also the known at first hand, and the unique the individual's point of view.

Commenting on a piece of descriptive writing entitled 'A Windy Day', Frank Whitehead, in *The Disappearing Dais*, had this to say:

> This is for the most part 'correct' and 'acceptable' insofar as techniques are concerned; but it lacks individuality, and the writer's involvement in her subject-matter is surely no more than perfunctory. We cannot doubt that this girl has ability, and even perhaps a certain verbal flair ... but she has been led to believe, presumably in her primary school, that a certain kind of writing is 'officially' expected and so she dutifully shuffles her cards about to produce a winning hand. We feel that such phrases as 'having a fine game with our hair', 'brilliant carpet of leaves' or 'playful cloud' reflect this conventional conception of 'good' writing rather than any direct apprehension of experience. (Whitehead, Frank, 1966, p. 188)

In his comments Whitehead describes the girl's writing as having correct and acceptable techniques, the writer as having ability and verbal flair, but he then devalues these aspects of her work by going on to explain them as products of a particular system of instruction, contrasted with another sort of writing which would be the 'direct apprehension of (presumably untutored) experience'. So his view of writing hinges on a contrast between the natural and the acquired, the contrived and the directly expressed. His argument gains added weight from the fact that he is discussing a *child's* writing here, for one of the other recurring themes of Romanticism is that the child's vision is somehow on a par with the poet's: fresh, original, unique, insightful. It is only the garish trappings of society and culture which will overlay and obscure this view as the child develops:

> Shades of the prison-house begin to close
> Upon the growing boy.

To turn children into poets and writers, therefore, is to encourage them to express what they already know. In writing about what they already know they will write with more insight, and more sensitivity, which in turn will make their work of higher quality.

In various guises this set of attitudes (with the underlying contrast between the personal, the expressive, the natural, the good and the second-hand, the acquired, the contrived and the bad) turns up again and again wherever people are talking, writing, commenting on children's work. Take the opening paragraphs to Donald Graves's *Writing: Teachers and Children at Work* (1983, p. 3):

> Children want to write. They want to write the first day they attend school. This is no accident. Before they went to school they marked up walls, pavements, newspapers with crayons, chalk, pens or pencils ... anything that makes a mark. The child's marks say 'I am'.
>
> 'No you aren't' say most school approaches to the teaching of writing. We ignore the child's urge to show what he knows. We underestimate the urge because of a lack of understanding of the writing process and what children do in order to control it. Instead we take the control away from children and place unnecessary road blocks in the way of their intentions. Then we say 'They don't want to write. How can we motivate them?'

Or, at the opposite end of the school spectrum, this comment from the O level examiners: 'As usual the best writing was based on experience and personal response, the worst on TV's never, never land' (SUJB, 1985, p. 42). Not surprisingly, just as personal writing embodies all that is approved of, writing based on popular fiction embodies all that is disliked.

It seems as if we've always been marking in this way, but notions of what constitutes good writing and how you can encourage the young to produce it are as historically variable as anything else. To the humanist school-teachers of the early sixteenth century, for instance, the idea that good writing could be produced by encouraging an individual to draw on their own resources and so shape a unique performance on paper would have been laughable. For them fine writing was shaped through imitation: by studying the exact formal style of the best classical writers and memorising as well as translating specific texts, pupils could acquire the same skills. Thus one of the most important tasks allotted to diligent pupils was to amass their own commonplace books:

> From [the master's] reading the boys were to collect flowers of rhetoric i.e. antithesis, epithets, synonyms, proverbs, similes, comparisons, anec-dotes ... [the list goes on] (The Eton timetable in 1560, quoted in *The Changing Curriculum*, The History of Education Society (ed.), 1971, p. 3)

The point of the exercise was then to have those same phrases at your disposal when it came to your own writing:

> When a passage had been read and explained the next stage was always to memorise its more elegant phrases for use in other contexts ... your fully trained humanist had ready a dozen stock stories, a dozen stock generalisations to illustrate it. (Bolgar, R. R., 'Humanist Education and its Contribution to the Renaissance', pp. 16–17 in *The Changing Curriculum*)

The fact that pupils' writing can now be condemned as derivative, clichéd, 'straight out of a woman's magazine' (routine comments spattering the margins of my English Department's CSE essays) seems to suggest that pupils and teachers are operating under different systems: pupils imitating whilst teachers look for originality. Yet as the third term above implies, this sort of condemnation is reserved for those who are judged to imitate a particular body of literature – popular fiction. Would pupils be accused of being clichéd if they had carefully striven to write in the manner of Kafka or Virginia Woolf?

It is within this context that I want to place the sort of advice which teachers hand out to pupils when they are not seeking to improve their style, but their content: the advice to stick to what you know, concentrate on feelings, familiar situations, get close to your characters.

Not only does pushing pupils back in this direction seem one of the few places to go when efforts to help them write better in a detached and abstract way have failed (besides, it must be easier – Britton's developmental model of writing says so), but pushing children back to personal experience also becomes a certain way of avoiding the clichés of reproduction. The personal comes to stand for the individual, the unique, the spontaneous, the direct and to stand for them in opposition to the hackneyed, the stereotyped, the garbled, the second-hand, the already known, which come from a poor attempt at retelling – and especially retelling of despised popular fiction, which hardly deserves to be told in the first place.

The formulas borrowed from other texts come to be seen as exercising a stranglehold upon the imagination, forcing the creative outpourings of the child's naturally vivid imagination into narrow channels. If only children could be persuaded to return to the freshness of their own insights, untainted by popular fiction! We are treading on dangerous ground here: constructing an age of innocence, life before popular fiction set its mark upon it. We are back with the notion of the Fall, innocence before knowledge, the individual before social constructions, nature before culture. In other words, setting the problem up in this way takes us to the heart of a complex debate about where the individual is located in relation to language and culture. For what such a view (the contrast between the personal and the derivative) presupposes is that there is a moment or a place before, or outside of, the knowledge of (the wrong) story and that if children cannot be persuaded to draw on the right literary sources to improve their style, then the safest place to go is into themselves and their understanding of themselves before the sullying contact of the written word. What I want to go on to argue is that no such safe place exists.

To appeal for children's self-expression, their inalienable right to speak from the heart, suggests the possibility of their writing speaking directly about themselves, giving unmediated access to their lives. What such an argument ignores is that even 'the spontaneous overflow of powerful emotions' has to have form. You can't just scream or wail on paper. A personal piece of writing cannot be so idiosyncratic that it is unintelligible to anyone else. To qualify as a piece of writing at all, as an answer to an essay title, the piece must enter into a system of shared meanings and as far as a piece of writing goes that means

ing syntactically recognisable, but also obeying the rules
g itself. In other words, to ask children to write is always to
to write in a recognisable form. We acknowledge this in what
e to say about style: asking children to improve their style
means 'borrowing' from other literary texts, other forms of writing.
Even when we don't ask them to do this explicitly by handing out
worksheets encouraging children to sprinkle their writing liberally
with literary effects – metaphor, powerful adjectives, longer words –
this is the implied model. How else could children redraft, with what
in mind? Why else do we suggest they read more widely to improve
their writing? But personal writing is seen as an exception. The idea
here is that we can overleap references to other texts and get directly
to the speaking self, the presence of the author, their experience, their
self-knowledge. But the speaking self, in so far as it uses language, is
also already structured too. We can never get at the direct apprehension
of experience because we know that experience for what it is only
through the medium of language. Moreover, language is never the
property of a solitary individual, but a set of shared conventions,
shared meanings, which predate the individual – into which, indeed,
an individual is born.

If personal writing was really individual, unique, original, every
piece would be radically different from every other. But this is not the
case. There are recurring sets of conventions according to which we
judge whether a piece of writing is personal or not and how personally
felt it is. Thus a piece of writing in which a boy imagines himself
to be a U-boat captain fighting in the Second World War is not
considered personal. A piece in which a girl describes the uncertainties
and anxieties of adolescence, dwelling on her unaccountable changes
of mood, is. On the other hand, a piece of writing in which a girl tells
us about her sister by describing the colour of her hair, how tall she
is and then listing her current hobbies obviously is personal writing,
but it is not judged to be as personal as a piece which tells us of family
rows, conflicts and discontent. A boy who writes about violence on
the streets in the narrow back alleys near the chippy is deemed to be
telling it like it is: a girl who writes about an uneventful night at the
Brownies is merely boring (unless of course she manages to suffuse
the whole piece with the atmosphere of the place and dwell intro-
spectively on her feelings whilst she's there).

To write personally, therefore, is just as much to subscribe to a formal system of organisation as to write in a 'derivative' way. Formula writing simply underlines (rather than disguising) the fact that the author is using a *shared*, not private, notion of how a piece of work starts and ends, and what will happen in between. Far from considering formula writing as a temporary lapse, 'the first rung of a ladder' leading ultimately to somewhere else – the more mature, more serious response to art or subjects of importance – formula writing for me raises all the questions about what children are doing when they write at all, what mastering writing means and how far it might be implicated in the coming to terms with identity.

3

Texts and Values: The Power of the Book

Teachers can condemn children's writing based on popular fiction by describing it as derivative, a judgement whose negative value depends on an underlying assumption that good literature is the product of the individual's unique vision. Such comments are delivered when the work is complete and are made in the context of a teacher assessing and marking work. So I began by looking at the expectations which determine the kinds of work teachers set their pupils and the framework within which they pass judgement on it or seek to turn it in new directions. I went on to show the inadequacies of the contrast between the unique and the second-hand and to argue that in writing at all children are inevitably entering into and using a shared set of assumptions about what writing is. If they transgress the rules – hand in a piece of paper with the words 'Lee is King' written on it, for instance, when they have been asked to write about 'The Fight' – the teacher will not consider this a piece of writing at all: a doodle, a waste of time ('Well at least he was quiet'), but not a piece of writing. Any writing – no matter how personal – to be recognised as writing must share the features of other texts. Children's formula writing, writing that draws on popular fiction for its sense of content and structure, differs from their other writing only in terms of its model.

In arriving at this position I also pointed to the lack of serious comment on children's writing based on popular fiction. About the only attention it gets is the scorn of the examiners. In the educational debate on writing, such work is always overlooked. Indeed, the debate about good writing depends on the absence of writing based on popular fiction: once you let it in, all the criteria commonly used to evaluate work collapse. There is another question underlying these arguments that I now want to examine: why popular fiction is in itself disapproved of. For if children are penalised for imitating it too slavishly, they are also penalised because the model itself is seen as second-rate.

Whilst there is silence on the classroom production of popular fiction, commercially produced popular fiction has attracted some notice amongst teachers, even if only as a sub-category of a more broadly defined popular culture. Popular culture is a bit of a ragbag term. It can be used to assemble together under the same heading such diverse activities as watching football, eating fish and chips, listening to pop music, reading thrillers, going to the cinema and watching soaps. The *Fontana Dictionary of Modern Thought* runs the term together with the phrase 'mass culture' and explains it like this:

> *mass culture*. A culture – known also as *popular culture*, and usually contrasted with *high culture* – which is identified with those products produced primarily for entertainment rather than intrinsic worth, for artifacts to be sold in the market in response to mass taste, rather than patronage, and with items created by mechanical reproduction such as the printing press, gramophone records and art illustrations. (eds Bullock, A. and Stallybrass, O., 1977, p. 373)

This definition stresses one aspect of the organising principle behind the term: that popular culture is primarily the culture of consumption rather than production. People are entertained by the products devised anonymously for them rather than by creating their own entertainment. Another way of looking at popular culture is to look at it as the culture of the working class. Thus football chants, autobiographical narratives of working-class life, styles of dress associated with bikers or skinheads, ballads composed by striking miners, can all be treated as the phenomena of popular culture. Behind it all there lies a question of value: whether popular culture should be spurned in favour of high culture, championed as the authentic voice of the working class, or granted the possibility of equal aesthetic merit with other works of art.

How does this debate filter down through educational theory to influence classroom practice? One set of arguments – tracing its history back to Leavis, amongst others – sees popular culture as a disease which needs to be fought:

> Those who in school are offered (perhaps) the beginnings of education in

taste are exposed, out of school, to the competing exploitations of the
cheapest emotional responses; films, newspapers, publicity in all its forms,
commercially-catered fiction – all offer satisfaction at the lowest level, and
inculcate the choosing of the most immediate pleasures, got with the least
effort.... We cannot, as we might in a healthy state of culture, leave the
citizen to be formed unconsciously by his environment; if anything like a
worthy idea of satisfactory living is to be saved he must be trained to
discriminate and to resist. (Leavis, F. R. and Thompson, D., 1948, p. 3)

Popular culture stands in this argument in opposition to good
literature; the nature of the pleasure to be gained from popular culture
dulls its readers' senses and threatens to undermine their ability to
discriminate, to seek out good literature. The two are absolutely
distinct, and it is the moral duty of the good teacher to guide the pupil
to the latter, the source of greater wisdom and true knowledge. For
in this view literature is not only aesthetically of infinitely higher
quality than popular fiction, worthy of critical attention because of the
greater skill it displays, but it also gets to the heart of human experience
and, by its power to illuminate the truth, can teach readers how to
live:

Much has been claimed for [literature]: that it helps to shape the person-
ality, refine the sensibility, sharpen the critical intelligence; that it is a
powerful instrument of empathy, a medium through which the child can
acquire his values.... In Britain the tradition of literature teaching is one
which aims at personal and moral growth, and in the last two decades
this emphasis has grown. It is a soundly based tradition, and properly
interpreted is a powerful force in English teaching. (DES, *A Language for
Life*, 1975, pp. 124–5)

Popular fiction, popular culture (the assumption is) do not have the
same effect:

Comics and commercials, headlines and hoardings – these typify the
influences which are at work all the time bludgeoning or beguiling our
children into eschewing mental and spiritual effort and accepting the
satisfaction which is easy, immediate and ready to hand. (Whitehead,
Frank, 1966, p. 56)

Popular fiction contaminates because it deflects pupils from the quest
for self-knowledge and limits them to a narrow, repetitive and damaging view of the world:

we must try to help children to see through the spurious, the destructive, the shallow, the dishonest. If we leave them to find their own way we could be condemning them to be manipulated or to be cynical, for without something of quality to which to turn, the shrewd and honest mind which sees through the manipulation of the mass media is shorn of a sense of value, and thus of hope. (Allen, David, 1980, p. 130)

When it comes to writing, the same sort of process is seen to be at work. Children who use models provided by popular fiction short-circuit the most valuable aspect of the writing process – the opportunity it affords for meaningful self-expression, the chance to explore one's place in the order of things. Popular fiction provides ready-made and easy answers to the complex problems with which children could creatively wrestle as they write. So the argument against popular fiction is both a moral and an aesthetic one, its roots in Leavisite literary criticism. Firmly wedded to the notion that to read is to experience, the teacher's task is to provide the best sort of experience through offering 'good' literature. Attacking the media, exposing the crudity of advertising, sweeping popular fiction from the library shelves is thus part of a moral crusade which will send pupils out into the world enriched by a knowledge of great art, inoculated against the corrupting influence of mass culture.

Another set of arguments about the nature of popular fiction has been aired within a predominantly Marxist debate about the nature of ideology which has in turn fed into Media Studies, and so percolated down to schools. In this argument, popular culture is seen as the domain of pleasure for the working class under capitalism. Capitalism produces popular culture, which is then consumed by a passive working class, alienated from its production. So popular culture is seen to play an important part in ideology and the maintenance of hegemony. Subjecting it to critical attention will reveal the deep-seated power relations within our society which it embodies:

We needed a broader definition of culture to deal with the way the mass media shaped and guided our view of the world. The theorists gave us the concept of 'ideology': a concept which made questions like 'Is this good television or bad television?' seem redundant. In studying the mass media we were studying how the dominant views of our society were reproduced again and again and again. (Bethell, Andrew, 1984, p. 220)

The view that popular culture is suffused with false images which effectively brainwash its consumers and should be treated as myth passing itself off as nature gave a new focus to the work of teachers committed to social change:

> I shall try to show how we can ... reinvest the notion of 'resistance' with its broader political meaning. Not resistance to the cheapest emotional responses, but resistance to those dominant values which deny social change and undermine human dignity. (ibid.)

The teacher's task here is to undermine the pupils' unreflective consumption of popular culture by demythologising the processes of its production:

> emphasis[ing] the constructed nature of the representations projected, and mak[ing] explicit their suppressed ideological function. Such an education will also necessarily be concerned with alternative realities – those constructions implicitly rejected, suppressed or filtered out by the images that appear. (Masterman, Len, 1980, p. 9)

In this passage Masterman is talking about television, but much the same attitude has been taken towards other media. Interest has centred particularly on images of women in advertising and the newspapers and on teenage girls' and women's magazines; with discussions of the problems in terms of sexist bias and stereotyping and attempts made to provide alternative, positive images of women. As far as children in schools go most of the attention in this argument has focused on the effects of consumption of such images and the ways in which they can be counteracted. Children are seen primarily as consumers, whose passivity in the face of texts needs to be shaken.

There are some interesting parallels in these two approaches. In both accounts popular fiction is viewed with suspicion. Its effects are judged to be both powerful and harmful, its consumers constructed as powerless to resist without teacherly intervention. Moreover, in both sets of arguments attention is focused on pupils as passive consumers of such fictions, not as active (re)producers. The main difference between these positions lies in what you do with the knowledge that popular fiction is potentially harmful. The first argument constructs consumers as powerless to resist without the development of critical skills fostered by careful teachers. Those who are saved will be more finely tuned to the richness of life. Thus for David Allen, engaging with popular culture means not

> merely criticiz[ing] it, or worse still, criticiz[ing] our pupils for watching it. The most fruitful approach is by encouraging in discussion a discriminating habit of thought, by helping a child to develop a set of criteria that sees the good as well as the bad. There are good qualities in some popular media, especially on television or in film. We should encourage children to see the good and to widen their range from among what is available. . . . It is not . . . our main purpose in English to be 'anti' anything. It is to be *for* the good things in life and in literature, *for* the good things in our children. (Allen, David, 1980, p. 130)

The second argument constructs consumers as victims of the dominant ideology which, by purveying false stereotypes, binds them to acceptance of a particular way of life. By examining how the media construct the images they purvey, and by putting forward alternative images, pupils can be shown the narrowness of the boundaries which confine them and will subsequently break out into new courses of action:

> Alongside critical analysis of media products it is important to give pupils examples of alternative representations of women provided by magazines such as *Spare Rib* and the occasional television programme, which allows space for women to challenge sexist assumptions. It is also important to explore the possibilities for challenging images directly. (Hunt, Philippa *et al.* (eds) *The English Curriculum: Gender*, p. 63)

What is striking about the arguments I have been describing are the terms in which hostility towards popular culture is expressed. There is the language of sickness: 'disease', 'healthy', 'inoculate'; the language of physical sensation: 'immediate pleasures', 'satisfaction', 'consumption'; and the language of power and powerlessness: 'brainwash', 'suppressed', 'harmful', 'confine', 'dominant', 'passivity', 'victim', 'resist', 'challenge'.

What is not allowed for in these arguments is that those who consume popular culture actually enjoy it. I don't mean that these arguments don't recognise the facts; they do, they return again and again to the question of pleasure; but they do so in curiously prudish terms. Looking back again at the passage from Leavis and Thompson, we have 'cheapest emotional response', 'satisfaction at the lowest level' and 'the most immediate pleasures'. This is the voice of the morally censorious approaching the subject of sex! They recognise the pleasure but simply wish that the people who indulge in it (who, after all, are never ourselves) would stop doing it. Great power is attributed to pleasure, a power greater than force, yet it is curiously seen as working in the same way: to control and subdue. Moreover, those who succumb to pleasure are seen to be doing so mindlessly. They surrender themselves to it. It acts upon them. How does this square with educational theories of reading which acknowledge that readers must actively involve themselves in constructing meaning from the text?

There is another set of arguments about popular culture which accepts more readily the pleasure that is involved and doesn't simply condemn it. This has been voiced within studies of male youth culture. Yet there is an ambivalence here, too. Pleasure can be accepted if it is also seen as a point of resistance. So the argument goes that in adopting their own subcultural mode (and realising its pleasure), young men are able to refuse their allocated point of entry into middle-class society, which they recognise, anyway, as a sham. Such behaviour is therefore justified and to be heartily endorsed. Yet the authors who scrutinise such activity (middle-class academics) also feel the pleasure and write about it lovingly, never pausing to examine their own response. Are they vicariously resisting too?

> The roughness and intimidation of the motor-bike, the surprise of its fierce acceleration, the aggressive thumping of the unbaffled exhausts, matches and symbolizes the masculine assertiveness, the rough camaraderie, the muscularity of language, of [the bikeboys'] style of social interaction. (Willis, Paul, 1982, p. 286)

There is much here which has been overlooked.

The debate about popular culture circles around questions of pleasure and power. Mesmerised by the texts or the products which produce pleasure, commentators overlook the interaction of text with consumer. If it is to be studied at all then it is always someone else's interaction that is observed – someone who is assumed to be more mindless, less rational, less capable of resistance than the observers themselves. Within this scenario teachers assume a passive wholesale swallowing of popular culture by their pupils. The teacher alone, long since inoculated against its debasing effects, can offer a way out:

pleasure can be subdued by rational argument and the almost physical sensations of uncritical enjoyment can be replaced by the cerebral detachment of a critical reading. The outcome: changed lives.

Media Studies are increasingly moving away from using 'popular culture' as their principal term of reference and instead organising what they have to say around another set of reference points: institution, genre, representation, audience. Suspicion or outright hostility towards the objects of study are no longer so central to the discussions as questions of value are more often replaced by questions about how meaning is achieved. The argument within English about reading has changed too: moving from a concern for the values texts represent to a point where the reader, not the text, is central to the debate. Now each reader is seen to be creating their own meaning from texts, and this rather than learning to decode is what becoming a reader is thought to be all about. Within this perspective it is harder to take an absolute line on the worth of any one text; its worth is dependent on what the reader makes of it rather than on any absolute quality it embodies. Once again, questions of value are dropping out of sight. However, neither of these two shifts in perspective means that teachers are explicitly promoting popular fiction. Question marks remain, along with a certain amount of unease about the change in perspective.

Perhaps we've got to the point of tolerating popular fiction not because it's where we planned to go but simply because that's where our pupils have led us. We'd tried getting them to see how they were being manipulated by their favourite television programmes, debased by their comics and magazines, and they refused to believe us, or to change their reading habits accordingly. Even when they were prepared publicly to rehearse the teacher's views – 'Yeah, these comics are rubbish, Miss' – they nevertheless clung obstinately to their tastes and went on reading the stuff with obvious relish.

So far I've shown how the reading of popular fiction has been treated with suspicion and pointed to ways in which that suspicion is being replaced by other concerns within Media Studies and the arguments in English about reading. However, I want also to stress that there is one area of educational debate where suspicion and hostility towards the text remain as strong as ever: the anti-sexist and anti-racist perspective. Jane Leggett and Judith Hemming, in an article called 'Teaching Magazines', make this comment:

> In this period as the strength of the agreement behind the traditional ban on comics and magazines has weakened, among some English teachers the worry about the potential effect of comics and magazines has, paradoxically, deepened ... now [there is] a new inflection of that old worry: an awareness that the *fundamental* messages of these publications reflect and reinforce sexual stereotypes.... The messages are ... extremely stark when you start to see them ... they permeate practically every page, pictures as well as text; and any English teacher committed to tackling sexism in the popular media cannot ignore their influence. ('Teaching Magazines', *The English Magazine*, no. 12, 1984)

There is a wealth of material available on sexist and racist texts, how to spot them and what to do about them. In Rosemary Stone's *Pour out the Cocoa, Janet* (1983) the longest section is entitled 'Questions to ask about children's books' and begins: 'The following questions are to help teachers, librarians and other book selectors recognize the manifestations of sexism in children's books – from obvious stereotyping to less obvious, more covert bias.' Gillian Klein's *Reading into Racism*, a study of racism in children's books, has chapter headings such as 'What is a biased book? Recognition and responses'; 'Negative bias – does it matter?'; 'Strategies for Combat I: Sanitize or sensitize?'; 'Strategies for Combat II: Censorship or selection?' Numerous articles are available written by practising teachers, critical of existing texts and documenting strategies for coping with this sort of material. The collection *Alice in Genderland* (NATE, 1985) provides one example. Interest in the debate focuses on the impact of sexist and racist texts on their Black and female readers, who are judged to be at particular risk of being harmed by such texts:

> Stereotypes *are* belittling, especially if they are the only representations of females present: books solely about boys do *not* give 'full credence' to the 'seriousness' of girls' 'predicaments', and consequently [girls'] confidence in themselves and their future is not promoted. (Baines, Bridget, 'Literature and Sex-bias in the Secondary School English Curriculum', in *Alice in Genderland*)

Some concern is also expressed for white boys, though they get much less attention in the debate:

> It is important to realise that the rigidity of sex-role stereotyping is not only harmful to girls. Boys may feel equally inhibited by the pressure to

appear brave, fearless and smart if they see no other role models in books.
(Harland, Linda, 'Why doesn't Johnny skip? Or a look at female roles in
reading schemes', ibid.)

Concern is a key concept here. Anti-racist and anti-sexist teachers
are very concerned about what is happening to their pupils as they
read, whether their self-confidence and sensitivity are being nurtured
or undermined. They are preoccupied not just with the value of
particular texts as they are being read, but with the way in which
particular texts may influence the personal well-being of pupils and
the direction in which they live out their lives. Texts are seen as having
an important part to play in the way children grow into mature
adulthood, and the people they become. This concern for the way in
which texts influence 'personal development' is there in the Leavisite
and Media Studies arguments with which I began this chapter. It is
also part and parcel of the more general concern in English for who
pupils are, who they might become. For the task of English as a subject
is first and foremost to contribute to this process of becoming.

Of course, all curriculum subjects make claims for the benefits they
can offer to the development of the child as a whole; but when it comes
to actual practice most subjects are committed primarily to handing
on a particular body of knowledge or set of concepts. This is what
takes up the time in the classroom. English is different. Certainly there
is a set of skills which is seen as the domain of the English teacher:
the mechanics of reading and writing. But these form a limited hier-
archy. This body of knowledge does not change radically as children
grow older: what is taught in primary school is not so very different
from what is taught in secondary school. Contrast this with what
happens in science or languages. In the absence of a particular
body of knowledge to concentrate on English teachers start the other
way round, not with the subject but with the subjects: the pupils
themselves.

The best of English teaching has always recognised the validity of the
child's experience. It has also understood that children are not vacant and
passive recipients of knowledge; they must engage actively with the business of English, and bring their experience of language and the world to
bear on it, in order for successful, enjoyable and worthwhile learning to
happen. (Hunt, Philippa, et al. (eds), The English Curriculum: Gender,
p. 5)

What the child brings to the English lesson is as important as what the teacher provides. English teaching becomes a way of harnessing children's own interests, developing them, deepening them and pointing them in new directions. So when it comes to reading, certainly up to the age of sixteen, the emphasis is not so much on acquainting children with a body of texts: the modern novel, the war poets, children's literature of the last decade – though these may of course be covered – as in exploring a set of themes. So reading *The Eighteenth Emergency* leads to work on bullying; *Under Goliath* to work on prejudice; *Of Mice and Men* to work on loneliness and friendship; the war poets to study of the misery and bitterness of war. Indeed, in many English Departments the primary means of organising work is around these themes themselves. The half-term's theme becomes the starting point, and the English teacher collects together a variety of resources which will illuminate it, from poems to plays to worksheets and written tasks. What is on offer is a personal exploration of the topic. Quite what the topic is varies, depending amongst other things upon the resources available, the way any one department is organised and the interests of the teacher, but many of the themes will concern what might be called moral, political or social issues (the label altering according to perspective). Texts may be considered good or bad according to the extent to which they confront children with the key issues and make them think through their own views again.

So I am arguing that what unites the differing approaches of the Leavisite tradition and of Media Studies to popular fiction, the anti-sexist, anti-racist perspectives on books and the more generally favoured reading practices in English as a whole, is a common concern for the development of the whole child and an assumption that the text is crucial to that development. Of course, different teachers will have very different priorities within this framework. For the teacher primarily interested in the quality of literature there can be personal benefits from reading the right text at the right moment:

A short story like 'The End of Something' by Hemingway can link up with specific, felt concerns and interests of pupils between the ages of fourteen and sixteen with their curiosities about boy/girl relationships, splitting/breaking up, the difficulties of loss, grief and separation, and (besides the local fascination with the details of a fishing trip), personal choices about identity, for example, the questioning within Nick about

> whether he is a person who needs to concentrate on hunting with Bill, or loving with Margorie. (Jackson, David, 1983, p. 17)

For the teacher primarily concerned with deconstructing the media, the wrong text read without the right critical strategy can be personally damaging:

> My worst problem is Astrid. She looks, actually, very like the blond heroines of the comic strips, her self image is clearly bound to the things we seem to be attacking. She sits at the front of the class and says, literally, nothing. She may file her nails, or just stare: I'm really worried about her. (Williamson, Judith, 'How Does Girl Number Twenty Understand Ideology', *Screen Education*, No. 40, 1981/2, p. 82)

On the one hand there is a concern for the impact of the text on the reader, on the other the nature of this concern determines the reading strategies to be adopted. If your priority is the exploration of the nuances of feeling which are seen to underlie the common experience of humanity, you'll want to involve children in the text, give them that finer experience vicariously. If your priority is to free children from the harmful effects of the hidden power relations within society, release the reader from its way of seeing, you'll want to deconstruct the fabric of the text and enable the reader to challenge the assumptions it embodies.

> The most effective and lasting strategy for combating racism and sexism and other damaging bias in books is to teach children to challenge everything they read. They need to learn to doubt the messages of the media and to develop and ultimately to trust their own judgement. (Klein, Gillian, 1985, p. 113)

My argument is that whichever approach is adopted, teachers hope to influence the sort of people their pupils become by getting them to read particular texts in particular ways. Texts are chosen not so much for their intrinsic merits – their stylistic qualities, their turns of phrase, the elegance of the language used – as for what they can *do* for pupils.

If I am right in arguing that concern for the personal development of pupils lies at the heart of much English teaching, then this concern will inevitably have repercussions on the way in which we deal with pupils' writing. At the end of the first chapter I drew attention to the way in which personal writing, rather than being an area in which pupils are free to write anything they like about themselves, is actually quite narrowly defined, and that definition presupposes a particular relationship between writers and their texts – namely that writing can directly reflect the writer's experience. I drew attention to the prevalence of what I characterised as the Romantic view: that at its best writing actually embodies the experience of the writer, in a direct and unmediated way. Such a view of the relationship between writers and their texts leads teachers to give priority to personal writing and – within that category – to writing which dwells on a particular structuring of feeling: subtle, uncertain, full of doubts or angst, provoked by conflict, yet where each side of the conflict can be seen, and so remains unresolved. This structuring of feeling is assumed to be open to anyone if they only pay close enough attention to themselves, and the dividend for feeling in this way is that you gain access to a mature vision of the complexities of human experience.

Such a view also leads to the teacher's attempt to inculcate particular sensibilities in the writer. For the assumption is that if you write well about your experience, it is because you have felt that experience deeply; if you write badly then it must be because you have paid insufficient attention to what has really gone on. To write (and to read) well is therefore to become a particular sort of person, sensitive to a particular sort of experience in your life. If you are not writing well, you are denying yourself the possibility of that sort of experience; you are *being* a different sort of person. If the teacher's job is to encourage children to develop a particular set of feelings in their writing – questioning, uncertain, aware of subtleties of emotion – then aren't they also, in the process, inevitably influencing how the writers see their lives?

Of course, not all the concern will show itself in these ways. Just as there are disagreements over what are the best ways to encourage children to read, which are the best texts for the teacher's purposes, so there are disagreements over what to do about their writing. Nevertheless, there is a consensus that in judging writing, besides looking at the mechanics – spelling, handwriting and punctuation – or style, we can also judge something about the writers: who they are, and what they are able to say about themselves. The strength of our concern depends on the extent to which we judge the writer to be present in the text. At one extreme is the work of David Holbrook, who treats texts as direct reflections of the psychological well-being of their author, insisting that much of children's writing is a cry for help, and that the teacher's role is to act as therapist. If we are less certain about the relationship of the text to the writer, our worries may be much vaguer. Does the fact that a piece of socially realistic writing, handed in for homework, deals with drinking and violence in the home mean that the girl who wrote it has first-hand experience of this and that we should be worrying about her? Does the fact that a girl consistently presents her stories in the first person, the voice that of the male protagonist, mean that the author is refusing the space alloted to femininity by patriarchy, or that she has an identity crisis on her hands? Does the fact that a girl's romance story culminates in two girls fighting over the boy of their dreams suggest an unhealthy preoccupation with the value of young boys at the expense of the values of female friendship? Does the fact that a boy's stories frequently include violence meted out to his women characters, who end up seriously wounded or dead, imply that he is a sexist monster committed to abusing women in his own life, that he has a difficult relationship with his mother or a problem with his (female) English teacher?

Such questions about texts are inextricably bound up with questions about the writer, but if this is the form our concerns take it is harder than when dealing with reading to know what line of action to pursue. Those who have most clearly conceptualised the relationship between text and author, as indicated above, are also the most certain about what to do. What are the options for the rest of us? What should our response be? Do we pass on the information we may feel we have gleaned about an individual to their Head of Year, or someone else with responsibility for pastoral care: match their knowledge with our own? Do we have a quiet word with the individual concerned, or perhaps ban certain sorts of writing – 'this is not acceptable' – in the hope that they will move on to better things? Or do we remain vaguely worried and do nothing, except perhaps to review the sort of reading we offer the class? We are unlikely to suggest that writing in a different way will in itself solve the problem.

There is another point I wish to draw attention to. Our concerns about boys' and girls' writing are often differently framed and differently expressed. One reason for this is that teachers' worries about girls and boys are often informed by the anti-sexist perspective. I've been using the term 'anti-sexism' so far rather than 'feminism' because I do not consider the two to be synonymous. The anti-sexist argument can be a feminist argument but it can also be reformist, or even misogynist. As examples in the latter category I would put statements like the following by Bob Dixon in *Catching Them Young 1: Sex, Race and Class in Children's Fiction*:

> Since girls in general are so severely conditioned and repressed and so turned in upon themselves, they fall victims to fantasies in consequence. (p. 13)

> In fiction for the very early years, we saw the cage being built. More and more now, women will take the task upon themselves, in fiction as in life. Most grow up believing that the role society has set out for them is a 'natural' one, innate and inborn. This process, by which the oppressed takes on – internalises – the attitudes of the oppressor, is a well-known one. (p. 6)

> [Girls'] active lives, as we've seen, are much more restricted than boys'. Therefore they tend to live substitute lives, and, increasingly, dream lives through fiction. (p. 4) (Dixon, Bob, 1977)

The position Dixon puts forward in his book, however well intentioned, smacks too much of 'blame the victim'. Behind what he says lurks a considerable contempt for the women who fall prey to sexist ideology.

The anti-sexist argument draws, therefore, on a particular set of attitudes which not all of us who are feminists would want unquestioningly to endorse. Indeed, I have several reservations about the position. At the moment, however, I want to concentrate on what the anti-sexist argument has to say about the relationship between texts and the formation of identity. One of the crucial questions for anti-sexism is about who readers identify with when they read. A contrast is drawn between the opportunities open to boys, who are seen to be presented with a wide range of roles, offering the possibility of full identification for the male reader; and the opportunities available to girl readers, which are seen to be much more heavily circumscribed. Female characters are often missing altogether from the reading schemes and children's books berated by the anti-sexist lobby, and when they *are* present they are often portrayed in a negative light. So, the argument goes, full identification with the characters in the book can be bought by the female reader only at the expense of negative self-image. What happens to girl readers is therefore compared to what is assumed to happen to boy readers. What is assumed to happen to boy readers – full and positive identification with the text's characters – is also assumed to be a good thing, which girls are being unfairly denied. Without the reassurance of an accurate reflection of who they are, girls are considered to be at special risk of being harmed by texts. Indeed, in some forms of the argument the possibility of identification with a positive and realistic representation of the self is regarded as a prerequisite for psychic wholeness.

Boys are seen to be getting a bad deal out of their reading experience when they are assumed to be victims of the same sort of unrealistic stereotyping that affects girls; only this time the stereotypes are reversed and it is the obsession with the macho, go-getting, aggressive aspects of masculinity which are seen to damage otherwise more sensitive types:

> Offering boys fiction with independent and self-sufficient female characters is undeniably important as a means of teaching boys about girls, but a further and equally important need is to teach boys about themselves. The sort of boys I mentioned earlier, who are not natural members of the macho club, are not well represented in much of the fiction we read in schools. If they are depicted it is often as outsiders or victims rather than people with positive and important strengths. (Stephens, John, 'If it's fragile it must be a girl', in *The English Curriculum: Gender*, p. 113)

No one assumes that boys are getting a bad deal because of the possibility for full identification itself. Yet I wonder about that. After all, the possibility of fully recognising yourself in the text hardly seems to turn boys into well-balanced anti-sexist men.

There is another problem. The argument compares what happens to girls as they read with what happens to boys. The assumption is that boys' experience is the norm and that girls' experience is therefore lacking. Even when an analysis of girls' difficulties in reading is based on the observation that such difficulties stem from the male values that the text embodies, the next move is usually to look at how girls internalise those values. So attention is deflected from scrutiny of male power to the assumed powerlessness of girls. Girls, the victims, come to be seen as the problem which needs curing; boys, the oppressors, escape from view. I am reminded here of what Susan George, in another context – writing about the causes of world poverty and hunger – has to say about the comparative merits of studying the powerful or the powerless:

> Here comes one of the most important sentences in this chapter: *study the rich and powerful, not the poor and powerless.* Any good work on peasants' organizations, small farmer resistance to oppression, or workers in agribusiness can invariably be used against them.... Let the poor study themselves. They already know what is wrong with their lives and if you truly want to help them, the best you can do is to give them a clearer idea of how their oppressors are working now and can be expected to work in the future. (George, Susan, 1976, p. 289)

How clear an idea do we have at the moment of how boys work?

On the whole, when it comes to their writing, those aspects of boys' work which are most likely to concern teachers are the outright expression of sexist or misogynist views. In other words, boys writing about attacks on women or boys who incorporate women into their texts as crude sex objects are most likely to have their work challenged and rejected in no uncertain terms by the teacher. A student teacher told me recently of a classroom where she'd been working where one of the boys involved in producing a group magazine had written a letter for the problem page purporting to come from a rapist who enjoyed what he did. On discovering the document, the class teacher ripped up the piece of work and bawled the child out. It became obvious from the student's description of this incident that the boy, for all his self-justificatory howls of indignation (or maybe because of them), had been deliberately winding the teacher up. She was, of course, female. What is interesting about this is that when I have under similar circumstances challenged boys about their work – once about a story which culminated in the shooting of a Pakistani family, once about the inclusion in a piece of work of explicit sexual activity – the boys concerned accepted with hardly a murmur my assertion that such writing was unacceptable. Their personal investment was not so much in the text and what it said about themselves as in their apparent desire to annoy or embarrass me: an important difference. Apart from that, no concern is expressed at the fact that few women in any shape or form, whether as mothers or girlfriends, get anything other than a bit part in texts written by boys, who seem to exist in an all-male environment when it comes to their writing. Nor do teachers waste much time worrying about the preponderance of a limited repertoire of genres in boys' writing, a repertoire which favours action at the expense of emotions: sci-fi, thrillers, sports stories, in all of which the relentless theme is one of conflict with the outsiders, the aliens, the other side.

When it comes to girls' writing, a different picture emerges. After all, there is much more to worry about once you accept the notion that girls' identity, their self-image, is at risk unless the text, whether read or written, offers them a true reflection of themselves. We can worry about girls' absence from their own stories, we can worry about their presence within the text, whether it shows them in a positive light or not. We can worry about their self-confidence as writers. Commenting on a project on autobiography which she started with a first-year class of girls, Hazel Taylor writes:

> the most important aim in choosing autobiography was to tap the sources of personal experience within each child. This I hoped would lead, through the recall, selection and evaluation which would be demanded by the writing process, to an increase in self-esteem and a new sense for each girl of herself as someone with a separate identity. I feel this is particularly important for girls as they are often good either at writing stories about the adventures of others, through whom they vicariously experience them, or at personal writing which reflects the role of girl child as assistant or observer to the experiences of others. In an autobiography, the self is central. (Taylor, Hazel, 'Autobiography', in *The English Curriculum: Writing*, p. 82)

We can make out a case for girls' writing being in a male voice, but this needs working on:

> Though the girls who wrote the story are orientated towards education and could be said to be actively seeking access to educational discourses ... there is some evidence that they display a resistance within the production of an accepted discursive form: the use of the male working-class persona and the use of words clearly proscribed by the school tend to subvert the pedagogic limits in which their writing is almost enclosed. Furthermore by the assumption of a specifically male and aggressive style they may be seen as asserting a power resistance in one of the few available

forms. (Richard, Chris, 'Classroom Readings', *Screen Education*, No. 4,
1981/2, p. 74)

We can worry about the genre they use. If the most 'exciting' subjects –
the gritty slice of working-class life, the adventure story, crime – seem
to come complete with a set of male characters, what does that leave
girls to write about? If they are to include themselves, how can they
avoid being boring? By sticking to description? For even worse, in
many teachers' estimation, are the genres which revolve around female
characters: horse-riding, a slice of domestic life – 'An Evening Baby-
sitting' – worst of all, the romance. This is the most roundly condemned of all genres. It is disdained on the grounds that it reproduces
stereotyped images of women, reinforces the powerful status of men,
provides dangerously false pictures of the world and is self-evidently
rubbish anyway. In my English Department it consistently drew the
more virulent criticism. It is curious that romance should be isolated
in this way for particularly harsh treatment, but I'll return to this
point later.

We can even worry about the negative impact of anti-sexist teaching
on girls:

> members of the department feel that an approach to gender through
> Literature is more productive than 'doing it' as a theme. I agree with this
> general view. It avoids the 'Oh No! Not Again!' reaction of 4th/5th/6th
> year pupils who have 'done' sex-role conditioning in Social Studies and
> often feel attacked by teachers encouraging them to view frills, tea-sets,
> dolls and other aspects of their own childhood as 'wrong'. (Gaskell, Carole,
> ' "Frills, tea sets, dolls": reflections on teaching in a girls' school', in *The
> English Curriculum: Gender*, p. 117)

What I am arguing is that the girls in our classrooms operate as a
focus for our concern in a way that boys do not, precisely because we
see their grasp on their own identity, their self-image, as fragilely
constituted, in need of our support and intervention. There is a
paradox here. Whilst on the one hand anti-sexist teachers say that
books perpetuate a myth about girls being passive and helpless, on the
other they run the risk of subscribing to that myth themselves by
confirming that yes indeed, girls won't fight back until teachers show
them how. By worrying about all the negative pressures on girls and
their ability to cope, whilst insisting on the importance of our help,

aren't we turning them into the passive, helpless victims we came to save? Meanwhile, the security of boys' identity is not subject to the same sort of scrutiny, the same doubts. One of the worries with which I close this chapter is whether this is fair – to boys or to girls.

4

The Influence of Popular Fiction: An Oppositional Text

So far I have been talking about the concerns that English teachers bring to their reception of pupils' writing. These concerns are both for the form of that writing – the rules which underpin its production – and for the relationship of that writing to its author – what it tells us about who they are. I could put this second point in another way. Our concern for the relationship between text and author is governed by our concern for the production of good people, something which is at least as rule-bound as the production of their work. We have rules about what it means to be a good person, alive to the sensitive business of living; rules about what it means to be a good feminist, ready to take up the challenges of patriarchy. Our personal concern for children is played out against a background of texts. We look for children to produce texts of the sort we promote as offering the best versions of themselves. Identity, reading, writing are all somehow intimately connected, tangled up in the versions of English teaching we most commonly employ.

I am not sure that we have got the connections right. I've already argued that children's writing is not a simple, unmediated statement of who they are. What else might it be? What is the relationship between writing and the self? In what sense might we consider the author to be present in their own text (if at all)? What is the relationship between other texts, other readings, and children's own writing? The Leavisite, Media Studies and anti-sexist, anti-racist arguments propose that texts exert a powerful influence on writers both in the production of their own texts and in the way they live out their lives, and will inevitably do so without the application of critical skills which encourage distance from the text. Is this model right? Are we right to worry about girls so much and in particular to insist on the need for their full presence in the texts they read or write? Should we be more concerned about boys, and if so how could we show that concern without casting them as victims of the system in much the same way that we cast girls?

One way of beginning to answer these questions is to take another, closer look at some actual pieces of children's writing. This is what I propose to do now. All of the three pieces I examine were written for me by members of my fourth-year CSE/O level group at various points during the year. They were homeworks, but neither the titles nor the content were either chosen or guided by me, nor did they stem from any work we were doing in class – they were free choice! I hope to submit each piece of writing to close scrutiny. In this chapter I begin with a piece of work which derives much of its sense of shape and structure from popular fiction. It was written for homework by Angelique at the very beginning of the year that I taught her. In the following year, when I was no longer her English teacher, I interviewed her at length about her writing on three separate occasions and I will be quoting from those interviews later on. Angelique is Black, her school predominantly white.

In the reading of Angelique's text that follows my aim has been not only to mark the traces of familiar formulas as they appear in her work, but to examine how she uses these traces to shape her own meaning. It seems to me that the interest of the piece stems from the way in which Angelique puts her text together – a process of construction which relies not only on a knowledge of other texts, and their partial reproduction here, but also on her own experience and social knowledge. Within Angelique's writing these do not remain discrete categories but blur and melt into each other; in the process her own text establishes its own coherence. My reading seeks to re-create the coming into meaning of Angelique's text.

The piece is called 'Again!'

AGAIN!

'Why me though?', that's all I keep asking, why me? It all began when my mum had allowed me to go out of Bristol with a few friends, it wasn't usual but I ended up telling my mum what good friends I had and what they wouldn't do and what they would do (within reason of course!)

Anyway we took the train to London, Paul, Nick, Clare and me. It was hilarious on the train down. Nick and Clare had an arguement and Clare started throwing things at him. Paul and I walked out and Paul tried to get us a private apartment to get away from Nick and Clare but the man (him being a porter) said he didn't trust us, and wondered if we knew something of birth control. We just walked off into another carraige and sat down. Paul put his arm round me. I felt embarassed because an old woman kept staring. I shrugged him off, and kissed him when the lady had turned round.

'Wonder what Nick and Clare are up to?' said Paul looking closely.

'Probably tearing each others eyes out' I said. We both laughed.

At that Clare walked in. 'I wanna go home' she flopped on the seat next to the old woman. The old woman instantly walked out.

'Snobby bitch' remarked Clare.

'Oh Clare don't spoil the trip. We'll enjoy ourselves, we'll all go to the Fair' I said.

'Don't you two ever argue?' Clare said angrily.

'Well ... course we do' I smiled.

'When?' Paul asked me.

'Well ... loads of times' I said looking at him 'Why?'

'Nope, we've never argued' Paul said scratching his head, he pretended to be thinking.

'Yes we have Paul' I pinched him and gave him a 'Shut up' stare.

'Tell me when, then I'll shut up' Paul kissed me creeping around me slowly.

'Paul Richards and Angela Campbell give over' Clare butted in. We nearly got into a real fuss Paul and I did! Anyway, the rest of the journey is unimportant so I'll skip the rest.

We got off at Paddington.

Paul and I walked off into a café in London. It wasn't bad we had a sandwhich and a coke we started talking about the arguement we had.

'Paul we have had arguments before.'

'I know but I just wanted her not feel ... well ... never mind!' He never finished his sentence and I was hurt and upset when I asked him to finish he told me not to nag.

'What was going on' I thought to myself.

Nick appeared on the scene stuffing his face with a jam doughnut Clare just sat beside him sipping an orangeade.

'Bloody stupid cow you deliberately spilled that on me' Nick turned to Clare. Clare had spilt her drink on Nicks trousers.

'You sod, calling me a cow'

'Well you are one, who do you think you are?' Nick took a serviette and wiped his trousers.

'Look shut up you two' I said 'people are looking'

'Let them bloody look' Paul took my hand and lead me out of the café. We sat outside on the wall and kissed.

'I hope we don't ever fight like they do' I said holding his hand.

'Thought you said we didn't fight.'

'Well not recently' I argued.

'Yeah I know' Paul looked down.

I had been out with Paul before for two months but he left me and went out with Clare, yeah my friend, but we weren't friends then so it didn't matter much to me. I know I couldn't stand it happening again. Clare soon came out crying.

'Nick slapped me and he has finished with me' Paul instantly let go off my hand. He stroked Clare's cheek with his hand. 'Did he hurt you?' Paul asked.

'Course he bleedin' did' Clare sniffed.

'Bastard' Paul said.

'Paul?' I saw the way he looked at her the way he touched her.

'Paul? It's not over again is it?'

'I still love you Ange, I don't want to hurt you again.'

'No Paul No, you can't love her again?' But it was too late. He held Clares hand and walked over to the café.

Clare let go of his hand and shook her head. She turned her back on Paul and kissed Nick lovingly. Paul walked slowly back. He saw me crying and he held my hand, I let go.

'I'm sorry Ange I didn't mean anything' Paul tried to kiss me.

'No, No I won't let your last kiss remain a memory like the first one you'll only hurt me again I couldn't bear it I loved you Paul' I laughed 'probably still do ... but never Paul ever'.

Funny that evening, on the way home Paul and I sat apart, whilst Nick and Clare kissed.

*

'Why me though?' that's all I keep asking, why me?

The story opens with words spoken by the lead character, the narrator. It reminds me of the beginning of a photo-love story, with a close-up of the central character, establishing her mood through what she says. Angelique's story works on the same principles: the words spoken, a small action performed, focus my attention on the different characters. I can almost frame each separate picture:

> At that Clare walked in. 'I wanna go home' she flopped on the seat next to the old woman.

The first phrase would become the text in the corner of the picture, what Clare says would appear in bubbles and the picture would show Clare sitting on the seat.

> The old woman instantly walked out.
> 'Snobby bitch' remarked Clare.

The next picture would show Clare scowling as the woman leaves the carriage, the bubbles enclosing her remarks.

About the only passages which couldn't be packaged in this way are those which set the context of the story: the negotiations with Mum over whether the narrator can go up to London, and later on the information that Paul had once ditched the narrator for Clare. Each episode is self-contained, yet gains its full meaning by its relationship to the episodes which have gone before and follow after.

The narrator is obviously young – Angelique's own age. This is apparent in her relationship with her mum:

> my mum had allowed me to go out of Bristol with a few friends, it wasn't usual but I ended up telling my mum what good friends I had and what they wouldn't do and what they would do (within reason of course!).

This places the narrator as an adolescent, someone whose behaviour is of parental concern, who may be misled by friends into behaving irresponsibly; '(within reason of course!)' comments on the nature of the guarantees the narrator has given her mother and suggests both her independence and her acquiescence in her mother's concern.

I am continually reminded of the age of this group of friends throughout the story. Clare starts throwing things at Nick during an argument on the train journey down. This episode is preceded by the comment: 'It was hilarious on the train down.' The fight between Nick and Clare is not serious, therefore, just larking about. The friends are on their way to the Fair: ' "We'll enjoy ourselves, we'll all go to the Fair" I said.' When they arrive in London they go to a café and have sandwiches, Coke, a doughnut and orangeade. These concerns and interests belong to childhood. Childhood, adolescence, both create different contexts in which to read the characters' actions.

Being young also means being at the receiving end of adult disapproval:

> the man (him being a porter) said he didn't trust us, and wondered if we knew something of birth control ... an old woman kept staring

This sense of 'them and us' is part of a whole tradition of children's literature from *Just William* to *Grange Hill*. By tradition it can be a focus for stories. It is also part of Angelique's own experience, the stories she tells about herself. In her first interview with me she said:

> I wear my Dad's hats, and I wear shirts from my Dad's. . . . My Mum thinks I'm weird, and she thinks there's something wrong with me, she thinks I'm a lesbian, or something ... I think she's worried about me, you know. She thinks just because I wear my Dad's shirts or [laughs] something like that, there must be something wrong with me ... I combed my hair like, um, once I combed my hair. Do you know Grace Jones?

Gemma: Yeah ... oh yeah! [laughs]

Angelique: Oh, I'll never forget, I wouldn't never risk that again ... ever ... just to avoid argument, I wouldn't ever do it again.

There are two points I want to make about this extract, both of which have a bearing on Angelique's text. First, her comments arose as part of a discussion about sexism and the way it stops girls doing what they want to do. For Angelique the conflict with her parents is about what she may do as a girl. Her mother disapproves of her wearing her dad's shirts because it seems to signify an 'abnormal' sexuality. Wearing shirts may be natural for a boy; it is not natural for a girl. So what Angelique has to do to gain approval depends on an adult view of gender-appropriate behaviour. Youth is subdivided into girls and boys. The process of conflict and its resolution between adults and young girls is part of the latters' construction as female within our (patriarchal) society.

This notion that being young and female presents specific problems not shared by boys is there in Angelique's own story. At the beginning the narrator's mother worries about what the narrator will do if she goes out for a day with her friends. As she is a girl, this means worrying about sex rather than violence. The incident with the porter highlights this. The porter doesn't trust Paul and the narrator on their own. He imagines the presence of a girl and a boy means that they will indulge in sexual behaviour inappropriate to the young (rather than that they will wreck the carriage). When Paul and the narrator sit down together,

> Paul put his arm round me. I felt embarassed because an old woman kept staring. I shrugged him off, and kissed him when the lady had turned round.

It is the narrator as a girl, not Paul, the boy, who feels nervous about revealing the nature of their relationship in public, who can kiss only when the old lady is not looking. For her to be seen to behave sexually is to run the risk of adult disapproval, to be labelled promiscuous, common, cheap. It is girls', not boys' sexuality which signifies in this way.

This leads me to my second point: the extent to which it is possible to challenge the adult order. The extract I have quoted from Angelique's interview shows her contesting the adult's view of appropriate (female) behaviour but also, if need be, compromising – on her Grace Jones hairstyle, in this instance. But giving in doesn't mean utter submission. In her second interview I asked her about the differences in the writing she produces in school and the writing she does for herself at home. She talked about the difficulties of writing in patois in school:

> I remember doing a thing on what I liked for English, for Mr H— and, it was writing about stories and what I've achieved. I wrote this story, and he said to me 'Well how will people like *me* be able to read that story' . . . you know [smiles] and that really got to me because the only way a person who wants to read patois, you must *know* a certain amount of it because how on earth can I go round starting to pick out the bits of patois and starting to try and abbreviate it cos it *is not*, it's not a foreign language it's just a slang. . . . I felt really, really mad about it . . . 'how would a person like me be able to understand that!' . . . I thought, well, there is one way a person like you could understand it, but I won't bother to write it down.

Holding back, not challenging the views of others, can be a way of escaping those views when you lack the power to challenge them directly.

Mixed in with the judgement by adults of young people's behaviour is the question of gender. Appropriate young female behaviour is different from young male behaviour. Angelique's text shows that she is aware of this. Within her story, how does the narrator, a girl, react to this sort of pressure on her behaviour? She concedes to the adult view and does nothing whilst the old lady is looking at her; as soon as she looks away, she kisses Paul. For the narrator, a girl, behaving as she wants to means finding a space in which to do so, a space cleared of others' readings of her actions.

I began my analysis of this story by commenting on the similarities between the organisation of photo-love stories and Angelique's text in terms of the handling of dialogue and action. Photo-love stories take as their theme girl–boy relationships explored as romance. In Angelique's story the four friends are quickly established as two couples: 'Nick and Clare had an arguement. . . . Paul and I walked out.' Once their names have been linked in this way I begin to read the story in the context of romance. I expect the friends' focus of interest to be particularised, to be centred on their partner, their loyalties not to be to the group as a whole but to their special friend. My expectations are fulfilled as the group splits up: 'Paul tried to get us a private apartment to get away from Nick and Clare . . .', Nick and Clare's argument is private, between them as a couple. Precluded from joining in, Paul and Angela go elsewhere.

> 'Wonder what Nick and Clare are up to?' said Paul looking closely. 'Probably tearing each others eyes out' I said. We both laughed.

Paul and Angela are sitting peacefully with each other. They can guess that Nick and Clare will still be arguing. Paul and Angela become the steady, loving couple; Nick and Clare the bickerers who can't stop rowing. Points of comparison are established. But the arrival of Clare on her own breaks up the structuring of the group of friends as two couples, for Angela's attention passes to Clare. She is fed up – ' "I wanna go home" ' – and Angela's response re-establishes the group identity: ' "Oh Clare don't spoil the trip. We'll enjoy ourselves, we'll all go to the Fair".' Even if Clare is fed up with Nick, the day out need not be wasted; the friends can still have fun. Clare pushes the participants in the conversation back into their position as partners in a couple: ' "Don't you two ever argue?" Clare said angrily.' Her question stresses the difference between Nick and Clare, Paul and Angela: the former arguing, moody, unhappy; the latter content, calm.

There are two ways of viewing this contrast. Not arguing can mean security, trust, a perfect match, the perfect couple, by whose measure the other couple appear dissatisfied, ill matched, likely to break up. Or the calmness of those who don't row can tip into placidity, contrasted with the strength of feeling, the anguish of true love. Angelique plays with both images and resolves them in her final sentence: 'Funny that evening, on the way home Paul and I sat apart whilst Nick and Clare kissed.' The perfect couple, the couple who seemed likely to succeed – that is, end the story with a secure relationship – have broken up. The question the romance story asks about its key characters, the boys and girls who encounter each other within it, is: how will their relationship work out? To work out well the relationship must end intact, its stability secured, but for the moment this remains a question hovering above the text, guiding my reading. At this point in the story other considerations are also at play.

I want to return to the exchange between Clare, Angela and Paul and examine the different ways in which the dialogue of these three characters positions them. Angela has talked about the friends as a group of young people; Clare has placed them as two couples. Angela's response to Clare's moody discontent with her own relationship is to help Clare out. In order to try to stop her feeling gloomy about the rows between her and Nick, she suggests that her own relationship with Paul is just the same:

> 'Don't you two ever argue?' Clare said angrily.
> 'Well . . . course we do' I smiled.

Angela refuses to accept the polarity on which Clare insists. She offers friendship and a sense of solidarity. What she does is determined by how Clare feels; her own allegiance to Paul takes second place.

Paul's response is different:

> 'Nope, we've never argued' Paul said scratching his head, he pretended to be thinking.

He is still playing the couples game, reminding Angela of their status as a couple and scoring off Clare by showing her that his relationship with Angela is better than hers with Nick. For Angela, accepting his response will mean excluding Clare. She is caught between contradictory obligations – to her friend, to her boyfriend:

> 'Yes we have Paul' I pinched him and gave him a 'Shut up' stare.
> 'Tell me when, then I'll shut up' Paul kissed me creeping around me slowly.

Being in a couple means negotiating for what she wants, in a tight space, a space defined by others.

Angelique, the story-teller, is quite clear that in her romances what the boys want and what the girls want is often different, and part of the function of her stories is to settle that conflict. In her third interview with me she said:

> I think in my stories I really want the boy to be understanding. You always get these blokes that go off and two-time you and all this sort of thing ... every girl wouldn't want their boyfriends to do that ... the people I know they're always telling me that their boyfriend did this, and my boyfriend's hitting me about. ... When I'm writing my stories I want everybody to know that if I have a boyfriend my boyfriend ain't going to hit me about. If anything I'm going to hit him about.

Being in a couple means struggling over power.

In Angelique's story the struggle between Paul and Angela begins when Paul refuses to understand what Angela is doing (protecting Clare). His lack of understanding and reluctance to talk about it leave her hurt:

> He never finished his sentence and I was hurt and upset when I asked him to finish he told me not to nag.
> 'What was going on' I thought to myself.

She is on her own. The story continually fluctuates over where she is: safely inside a couple, her partnership assured by a touch, a kiss:

> 'Let them bloody look' Paul took my hand and lead me out of the café. We sat outside on the wall and kissed;

made to feel uneasy by that relationship:

> I felt embarrassed ...

> I was hurt and upset ...

part of a group of young people with allegiances to the group rather than a pair: ' "We'll all go to the Fair".' Angelique's story uses the formation of the group of friends into two couples as a starting point to do more than ask the question: 'Which couple will succeed?' By focusing also on the conflicting demands of the boyfriend and friend, by juxtaposing the different aspects of the group of friends, she can raise questions about what being in a couple means.

So far, in thinking about the presentation of girl–boy relationships in Angelique's text, I have examined the way in which the group of friends has been subdivided into two couples, and shown that this configuration brings with it the expectation that the story will centre around the securing or undermining of these pairs of relationships: an expectation which Angelique's final sentence, with its sense of symmetry, acknowledges. I have gone on to show how elements in her story undercut this tight focus and leave a space for other issues to be raised. What about romance? How does this figure in her text? The romance works by foregrounding emotions. Does the heroine love the hero, will he love her? Will the heroine be happy, her feelings shared by her lover, whose kiss promises a future together – or will she end the story bereft of her loved one, lonely, incomplete, sad? Either way, the romance can be filled with turbulent emotions, emotions which threaten to swamp the actions which generate them. Every gesture can become a sign of deep feeling.

Angelique's text is curiously empty of romance at the beginning. Paul puts his arm round the narrator, or kisses her, but her attention is elsewhere – on the old lady staring, or on Clare and her feelings. The one point the text offers at which they could become more absorbed in each other is quickly passed over:

'Wonder what Nick and Clare are up to' said Paul looking closely.

The phrase 'looking closely' spoken by a boy to a girl suggests a moment of intimacy, a move towards a romantic encounter. But Angela's response:

'Probably tearing each others eyes out' I said. We both laughed.

refuses this overture and re-positions the exchange as a moment of child-like glee. Angela's relationship with Paul seems domestic. There

is little sense of passion. She simply wants them to be comfortable
and at ease with each other:

> 'I hope we don't ever fight like they do' I said holding his hand.

Things begin to change as the misunderstanding between Angela and
Paul deepens. Suddenly inserted into the text is a brief reference to
Angela's past history of involvement with Paul and Clare:

> I had been out with Paul before for two months but he left me and went
> out with Clare, yeah my friend, but we weren't friends then so it didn't
> matter much to me. I know I couldn't stand it happening again.

Another way of reading what is going on emerges here. Paul has
already finished his relationship with Angela once. Do their present
conflicting interests presage another split, Angela to be left on her
own, alone, unhappy? The reference to Clare sets up other echoes by
reference to other texts. The girl whose best friend betrays her, seizing
the boy, causing heartache: a story in which the establishment of a
couple takes precedence over friendship, girls compete for the boy and
destroy trust in each other. But it is an echo which the narrator
summons up to dismiss: 'We weren't friends then so it didn't matter
much to me.' Her own action earlier in protecting Clare stands.
Nevertheless, the intensity of emotion with which Angela contemplates
being on her own – 'I know I couldn't stand it happening again' –
prepares the way for romance to enter the text. Romance reorientates
my understanding of what the characters do. It offers me a new way
of reading their actions as gestures become signs of deep feeling.

What is strange about this is that as romance enters, the coherence
of the text itself begins to shake. Suddenly all sorts of question marks
begin to hang over what is said. I find myself echoing Angela's 'What
is going on?' Part of the answer lies in the way romance is introduced.
It seems to sprawl in undigested chunks across the page. Precisely
because there has been no preparation for this sort of outburst, its
conventionalised nature stands out in high relief. Denaturalised, rend-
ered painfully visible, it spins away from the narrative confines of the
text that has gone before, refusing to be tied down by it, to stay in its
place.

I want to examine this part of the text closely from the point where
Clare comes out of the café:

> Clare soon came out crying.
> 'Nick slapped me and he has finished with me'

The row in the café has moved from the childish resonance of just larking about to a lovers' quarrel. Clare is no longer sulky, she is upset, yet the words she uses to describe how her relationship with Nick has ended still carry the child's view with them.

Paul's response concludes the switching of gear, true entry into romance:

> Paul instantly let go off my hand. He stroked Clare's cheek with his hand.

He caresses her, a gesture of intimacy and affection. It is also a gesture of exclusion: Angela stands outside this exchange with no role to play. Like Angela in her response to Clare on the train, Paul gives priority to Clare, the outsider; but because of the language used to describe his movement the gesture is positioned by romance, not friendship, and so speaks of his own self-interest, his claim on Clare, his desire to relinquish Angela in her favour.

> 'Did he hurt you?' Paul asked.
> 'Course he bleedin' did' Clare sniffed.
> 'Bastard' Paul said.

Again there is a contrast in tone. Clare obstinately refuses to shift into romance. Her answer reminds me of her youth. Paul's tone is that of the avenging male about to do battle with his rival for the girl's favour. He asks about Nick, not about Clare:

> 'Paul?' I saw the way he looked at her the way he touched her.
> 'Paul? It's not over again is it?'

Angela confirms my interpretation of Paul's actions within the framework of romance. Her words could have come straight out of a popular song. I don't have to be told how Paul is looking at and touching Clare. His show of affection triggers off the appropriate response in Angela: pain and grief, two moves in a sequence which leads to the disintegration of a relationship. Yet the next exchange is puzzling:

> 'I still love you Ange, I don't want to hurt you again.'
> 'No Paul No, you can't love her again?'

Paul counters the narrator's view of his actions but his remarks are swept aside: the narrator is the disappointed lover in full voice and immediately after Paul's declaration of loyalty to her the text confirms her view of him: 'But it was too late. He held Clare's hand and walked over to the café.' This could provide a convenient stopping place for the text: girl loses boy to the other girl, a tradition in which the other girl stands accused of betrayal and the heroine must accept defeat with tears. Angelique refuses this ending:

> Clare let go of his hand and shook her head. She turned her back on Paul and kissed Nick lovingly.

Angela's friend refuses Paul's offer and seals her rejection of him by kissing Nick.

> Paul walked slowly back. He saw me crying and he held my hand, I let go.

What is Paul up to? Trying his luck where he can, as Angela and Clare imagine, or helping out a friend? This time it is Angela who removes her hand, distancing herself from him:

> 'I'm sorry Ange I didn't mean anything' Paul tried to kiss me.

His excuse will not do. The language of romance has found him out, and pinned him down as the fickle lover whose words cannot be trusted:

> 'No, No I won't let your last kiss remain a memory like the first one you'll only hurt me again I couldn't bear it I loved you Paul' I laughed 'probably still do . . . but never Paul ever.'

Paul's return to Angela makes sense if this is still a story about childhood sweethearts, young people out for the day to enjoy themselves as a group, when no one's relationship is serious. Why not then talk of love to Angela and hold another girl's hand, comforting her? The language of romance has displaced the action, moving it away from the sphere of carefree youth to the world of maturity, passion, heartache, jealousy. In this arena lovers who betray each other's trust cannot return. Paul's route back to Angela is barred by her outburst. It draws heavily on the genre of romance. The fact that its meaning is hard to follow, that its relationship to the events that have taken place is awkward rather than clear, that its own message and tone are contradictory, doesn't matter. What it does is take the position of disappointed lover and turn it into one of strength. Angela, who has been deserted by Paul, now pushes him away. She makes the choice, she will not have him. In Angelique's hands the romance and all its attendant clichés turn the text upside down, confound our expectations. She ends the story with her heroine sad, but in control; alone, but determined to be so.

To summarise, Angelique's story interweaves several different, often contradictory threads: youth, romance, couples, friends, each of which evoke their own stories, lying beyond the text. They refer outwards, whether to other stories told in books – a literary tradition – or to the stories she tells about herself: her own experience shaped with others', formed through language. Reading her particular story I catch the references; and the characters, their actions, twist and turn as I place them within different contexts. The text seems to me not so much settled and secure as making up its mind, playing one thread off against another, shifting its ground. What emerges is a sense of the confined space within which the heroine, as a girl, has to operate: a space crisscrossed by contradictory demands made on her as a friend, girlfriend, lover. This sense of claustrophobia is not shared by the other characters in the story. Clare says what she likes and refuses to be swayed by others into losing sight of her own feelings. She takes risks – ' "You sod, calling me a cow" ' – but does so primarily by remaining childlike, obstinately moody. Paul pays no attention except to what he wants – ' "Let them bloody look" ' – but his single-minded purpose is selfish; he cannot be trusted to do anything except follow his own whims. Where does that leave those who care for him?

The juxtaposition of these varying approaches leaves Angelique's text uncertain. It is not the monolithic reproduction of a given order, a unitary whole, but fragmentary. It raises questions about what it might mean to leave childhood behind, to grow into womanhood and enter into relationships with men. On whose terms could this, should this, take place? What is at stake?

Angelique wrote several romances for me during the year I taught her. She refers explicitly to one other, called 'Oh Steve!!!' (see the Appendix), in her interviews. Although different in tone and setting, all her romances shared certain features. First, in all of them the girl ends up rejecting the boy – there are no happily-ever-afters; nor does the girl watch the boy walk out on her: she pushes him. Second, the boys themselves are not the focus for an unconditional surrender to the emotions on the part of the narrator – a common feature of the romance. There is always something about them that renders them ultimately untrustworthy and provides the motive for the girl to disentangle herself. Third, it is easy to read all these stories as if the narrator were white. Part of this is inevitably the effect of my reading rather than the text itself. For me (a white woman in a white culture) to read them otherwise, something in the setting or the language would have to mark the presence of Blackness. Unmarked, constructed within a form (romance) which I am familiar with, which brings with it images of whiteness, my expectations generate a cast of white characters. Yet this was not a feature of Angelique's writing as a whole. Increasingly during the year she brought in pieces of writing she was doing for herself at home, where the characters were explicitly Black and much of the language was patois. Why the difference in the romances she wrote for school? How far was she aware of the difference in her own writing? What do these differences suggest?

Angelique talked to me at length about her writing in the three interviews I did with her in the fifth year and it is to these interviews that I now want to turn. What quickly becomes clear from the transcripts is that here is someone who has thought hard about what being Black and female means, how it affects her own life. Answering my questions meant reminding herself of debates she had already had, as well as reflecting on them afresh:

> When it comes to the discussion on women, I always find myself getting annoyed because, I talk with my mother about this sort of thing and she seems to think a woman's place is in the home ... having to cook, clean and that sort of thing.

She introduced the question of race before I did. Explaining why her favourite programmes on television were 'No Problem' and 'Front Line', she said:

> I think it's just because it's lots of Black people acting. You hardly see any Black actors ... on the tele.

Gemma: Well, I was going to ask you about that, because when you were talking about the books ... quite a lot of the books

>   that you're talking about have got Black heroines ... and I
>   wondered if that was important for you, in terms of your
>   choice of book.
>
> Angelique: I think the reason I choose so many books by Black authors
>   is because of the school I'm in. There's hardly, I have never
>   seen anyone in this school pick up a book, no one has ever
>   done Black history in this school, so I look it out for myself....
>   If I was probably in a ... in a Black school, where there was
>   a high majority of Black, I probably wouldn't take much notice
>   of it ... – but – I think – once I'm in this school – and once
>   no one ain't going to teach me it – then I'll look for it myself.

She is confident in what she has to say, and articulate. I asked her
whether being Black or being female was more important to her, and
she was quite clear on her answer: 'I would say one's more important
than the other and that is because of being Black.'

How does this picture of Angelique as someone aware of the problems of racism and sexism square with her writing, and what does it
have to say about the status of her romances? Angelique accepts that
her romances are peopled with white characters and that to say this is
to say something significant: 'when you write about a white person, a
Black person, it's a completely different thing.' Pinning that difference
down, explaining it to me in words, was difficult and I didn't always
help to make the process easier. I raised the question in my first
interview and we pursued it in the second and the third sessions. I'll
try to bring together what Angelique said.

The sort of writing she does is dependent on the context within
which it is produced. The first pieces of work she showed me which
centred on Black characters were written at home primarily for herself,
although this distinction blurred during the year that I taught her,
and Black characters began to emerge in her school work. One of her
reasons for not introducing explicitly Black characters in her school
work is the reception she expects:

> I just know that if I start writing patois on a piece of paper, one of the
> teachers will come up to me and say 'What does this mean, what does that
> mean?' [...] I suppose it's normal 'cos they don't understand it, but I
> can't write patois in English because it's not patois.

In the teacher's eyes patois becomes incorrect use of English, but to make it correct, conform to the standard, would mean losing the flavour of the language, the very reason why she's included it.

Writing for herself at home means writing without constraints:

> When I write in my own stories I can just write what I want, you know, write patois, the Jamaican things ... and I can write anything I want even if it's not about Jamaica I can write something. Let the pen just run loose, you know, and really get across what I'm feeling on the book. In school you have to cut that down to a certain amount.

Even when race is on the agenda at school, talking about it means being careful, remembering her audience, not getting too annoyed: 'We talk about it in school, we talk about it in English, but, if I get too carried away, I have to control myself slightly.'

Writing for herself means being able to let go and re-create the Black world she left behind when her family moved out from the inner city to the white suburbs:

> When I left St Werburghs, I was really heartbroken because living on the street I lived on you could hear a West Indian mother opening the door and telling her son to get off the street because there's a car coming. You could smell the West Indian food cooking, the noise, you could hear a boy down the road playing his stereo unit from inside the house and that sort of thing. All those I really missed. I tell you I really missed them ... and listening to a bunch of Jamaicans talk ... specially the men when they get going. It's beautiful. When I moved up to Kingswood all that went. At first I didn't worry about it, nothing like that, but I started watching tele programmes like 'No Problem' and things like that and I really realised how much I missed it and I read the *Gleaner*, and that sort of thing and so I thought, well, I don't have it up here, I don't have that sort of thing at Kingswood, so I can *make* it happen so I started the stories and it brought it alive.

Her sources for this sort of writing are her own knowledge of the Black community and the stories they tell about themselves, and she is conscious that these ways of telling are specific to that community. Explaining a particular scene in one of her Black stories called 'Ebony and Ivory' where the mother can't bring herself to talk openly to her daughter, Angelique said:

> I think when it comes to talking love, romance, sex ... between an old-fashioned Jamaican parent, it's very difficult because they've been taught, when they were younger, that that's a no-no word, sex.

She went on to illustrate this point by recounting an anecdote about
her mother and grandmother. It is this sense of cultural difference
which explains why her romances centre around white characters: 'I
feel, I *do* feel, that Black people and white people act differently
when it comes to romances.' Her knowledge of how people behave in romances does not tally with her knowledge of the Black
community:

> They find it hard to express, Jamaicans anyway they find,
> most of them find it really hard to show loving, love and
> emotion. It's sort of like ... you know ... Jamaicans are
> supposed to be strong, tough, the guys anyway ... you know
> ... they told you ...

Gemma: I was wondering if that's what you mean when you say love,
            whether really what you're talking about is in a sense romantic
            love, yeah!

Angelique: Yeah! Roman, romance, yeah!

Gemma: It's like ...

Angelique: They're like that, they do, I mean ...

Gemma: ... being gentle.

Angelique: Yeah and gentle and kind. That sort of thing's not ... it's not
            ... the sort of thing ...

Gemma: ... the sort of thing ...

Angelique: that they sort of like *do*, you know ...

This sense of a difference in style is then picked up on and expanded
by her in a story she told about her aunt who, whilst shouting at her
son that he certainly couldn't have a bracelet she was wearing, was
taking the bracelet off and giving it to him: 'That's our way of saying
I, oh, I want to give it to you my love, ... my son.'

The register of romance finds different expression in the Black
community, whilst Angelique's acquaintance with the former has
been made through reading books which deal exclusively with white
characters. This affects her writing: 'I've never once read a Black
romance ... so I tend to write the stories as I have read in books.' To
position herself in a romance story, she also has to position herself as
white: 'Usually when I'm writing a romance, a story, it's usually just
me, but playing a white character, d'you know what I mean?'

The books on which she models such writing are exclusively white
and have little bearing on Black culture. To write a romance, therefore,

she 'plays' a white part. She followed up that comment by drawing a distinction between writing about Black and white characters:

> If I'm going to write something that's got to do with Black people then I'm really going to prepare it first, I mean I *think* about when I'm going to write something to do with a Black person yet when I'm writing something to do with a white person I just write it.

At this point in the interview I was confused. In a previous session she had talked about writing for herself at home as straightforward, easy compared to the constraints of writing in school: 'I thought I'm going to make it, so I wrote it out, do it, be how I feel.' Now she was talking about the ease of writing with a white voice, playing a white role.

Gemma: What I'm wondering is, when you say, when you're writing as a white person you just write, that would leave me, doesn't that mean you're writing more as you?

Angelique: Well, yeah, I suppose it does really but, I can't explain it really. I suppose when I'm writing as a white person ... it's more enough, I really just, it's all the books I've read. I've never read in my whole life really a Black romance. There's hardly any ones that I know actually. And so the ones I have read I tend to just write, sort of like copy in other words what they've written into my own type of words. I just write. With a Black romance there are certain things that you've got to get right.

The genre proposes white characters. To take the genre on board is to accept its setting. Alter the setting and she would have to alter the characterisation, the romance's exploration of events, its conventions. Yet it is these conventions she wants to explore – not, I would argue, at the expense of exploring her identity as Black, but alongside it. The simple reason for this is that the romance is the most obvious space in which to examine girl–boy relationships. This is one of the main reasons why feminists dislike it, but I'll return to this point in the next chapter. Support for this view comes from the way in which Angelique talks about her own romance writing. She has thought carefully about what she is doing and is involved in what she is writing. She consistently talks about the narrator-heroines in the first person:

> the girl, I end up saying, 'cos it's like me really the way I think I would act.... I end up saying 'Well you shouldn't have come running back to

me should you' really sarcastic but knowing in my heart that probably I
would really want this guy back.

But being involved doesn't just mean taking on board everything the
convention has to offer. She is critical of the form, both in what it has
to say about girls –

> I cannot, I hate reading a story where the girl's all 'Ahh', the Cinderella
> type of thing. It really annoys me because it's so stupid. That is the reason
> why we have so many stereotypes about women

– and the image it creates of boys:

> with the man with the most black hair and blue eyes, the irresistible blue
> eyes, the one with the blue eyes is supposed to be heartless and cold and
> the woman with the brown eyes is nice and warm, that sort of thing, it's
> really rubbish.

Instead, she works within the conventions to establish her own meanings: 'When I'm writing a story to me the girl has always got to be a
strong character.'

The problems girls encounter with boys in her stories are not to do
with whether they have a boyfriend or not but on whose terms the
relationship will be conducted, and here she places control in the
hands of the girl:

> If [the boys] start ... not being the way I want them to be in my stories,
> in my romance like they're begging me to come back to them, that sort of
> thing [smiles] I say 'No! I'm not going' and all this sort of thing and walk
> off.

It is the boys who have to put up with being powerless, cajole the girl
into staying within the relationship, and ultimately they lose. She
punctures the smooth and attractive pose in which they're presented
in the magazines:

> I done a description of Steve's room, page three all over the place, money
> thrown down where he's come home from work, his YTS scheme [...]
> his room looks a complete state ... that sort of thing, when I read a
> magazine all you see is ... hmmm ... well dressed, suit, nice tie, you know
> the sort of things that they write about, really rubbish [laughs].

To this extent she has adapted the romance genre to her own purposes.
However, as I've already shown, this doesn't leave her free to do

anything she wants. There are constraints, amongst them the question of how to end her stories. Romance offers two possibilities for closure: happy – the girl gets the boy of her dreams; or sad – she is left on her own. Either way the resolution is beyond the girl's control. It just happens, and it is final. Angelique's preoccupations, in particular with the wresting of control from the boy, fit uneasily within this format:

> I don't think there really is an ending in any of my stories

She comes to a temporary resting place: temporary because the solution is fragile, open to continuing negotiation.

> the last story I wrote, that Steve one, um, they ended up breaking up and him coming back to her and saying 'Oh will you please' and she's saying 'No, it's not worth it because you're only going to do the same thing to me again!'
> That's the sort of thing it is and then I pick it up again, if I feel like writing another story, sometimes we go out with each other again, sometimes we just don't bother … it's not worth it.

It is difficult to reconcile her conflicting desires: wanting the boy and yet not wanting to be dominated by him, used by him.

> I end up saying 'Well you shouldn't have come running back to me should you' really sarcastic, but knowing in my heart that probably I would really want this guy back.

The endings in her own stories are uneasy. They do not conform to the stark distinction drawn in romance (happy/sad) – the point they have reached is more subtle. But to think about them in terms other than those proposed by romance is hard.

> It was just the sort of ending where she was going to go off and find another boyfriend and at the time, *now* when you think about all this business about women being stereotyped and all this, *now* I think of it as a woman going off and having her own independence without a male tying her down, but then, I didn't think of it that way.

Gemma: Did it seem to you when you wrote it as a happy or a sad ending then?

Angelique: Sad ending, I think, well not sad ending but just that she wouldn't have Steve.

I have been attempting to map out in my account of Angelique and her writing a far more complex interaction between the writer and her text than the customary arguments about popular culture and popular fiction allow for. Angelique's writing cannot be understood in terms of entirely passive consumers hopelessly trapped and subdued by an all-powerful popular fiction, relentlessly undermining their perception of the real world. Angelique's romance writing is about modification, adaptation, transformation of the genre within which she is working. Her text exploits the contradictory ways of reading offered by her sources to open up new spaces and to pose her own questions about identity, emotion, power. If it is not the seamless text, the unitary whole which the argument about popular fiction assumes, the same holds true if her writing is viewed by the standards of good literature. I want to argue that it is precisely here, in its fragmentation, that its strength lies.

All this implies freedom for the writer. There are also constraints. Angelique's interview points to what is excluded in her writing for school, the difficulties of writing about herself as Black within that institution. The agenda of the romance is for her a partial one. But in saying this one further point must be borne in mind. She is very aware of her identity as a Black girl. Even without the pressures of the institution within which she writes, where would she look for a genre which addresses itself to both these issues? Her politics must take her into two separate camps. Whilst this may not be ideal, it is an inevitable result of writing within the culture in which she is placed and from which she must draw.

5

Romance and the Agenda of the Conventional Text

In looking at Angelique's writing I have shown that, although working within constraints, she is able to modify and adapt the formulas of popular fiction, using them to raise her own questions and to express her own purposes. I chose Angelique's text because her refusal to adopt the conventional ending of romance seemed clear. I interviewed her at length because I knew that the issues I wanted to raise with her were issues she had already thought about, and that she would have strong views on questions of sexism and race. Others in that class were more ambivalent, their own thinking less clear-cut, their writing outwardly more conventional. So is Angelique a limited case, a writer able to manoeuvre within the romance genre, perhaps precisely because as a Black girl she is inevitably partially excluded from it, distanced from its all-embracing totality?

This is one point which I want to pursue. There is another. So far, in discussing children's writing I have talked about it largely in terms of its relationship to popular fiction: a blanket term which in fact conceals a variety of genres. These are not treated equally. At certain points I have drawn attention to the way in which romance is singled out and dismissed in particularly strong terms. Thus Paul Hoggart, for instance, in his essay 'Comics and magazines for schoolchildren,' says of adolescent girls' 'magazines':

> These magazines have a preoccupation with the problem of finding and holding a boyfriend (a 'hunky fella') that borders on the pathological.

and

> The frame of reference is staggeringly narrow. (Hoggart, Paul, 1984, p. 145)

He makes no such comprehensively damning comments on sports comics, or any of the publications for boys he has examined. Perhaps this is symptomatic of a sexist society which denigrates all things female? But feminists too have found themselves in some difficulties when thinking about romance.

> Women's criticism of popular feminine narratives has generally adopted one of three attitudes: dismissiveness; hostility – tending unfortunately to be aimed at the consumers of the narratives; or most frequently, a flippant kind of mockery. (Modleski, Tanya, 1984, p. 14)

Modleski goes on to attribute such strong feelings to embarrassment. Certainly as far as feminist teachers go there is a sense of unease about using romantic fiction with their pupils.

> But slowly doubts began to creep in. It wasn't so much a question of what the books were about, as what they were *not* about. Was it right that we should be reading so many books with 'girly' subjects like romance and pregnancy? Weren't we just contributing to the idea that girls' lives occupy a special enclosed area in which war, aggression, adventure, sport, play no part? (Frith, Gill, in *The English Curriculum: Gender*, p. 13)

Unease relates to the agenda romance is seen to construct. It points girls only in the direction of love and marriage, restricts the possibilities for action to the quest for a boy. It is intensely individualistic.

> The Jackie Girl is alone in her quest for love; she refers back to her peers for advice, comfort and reassurance *only* when she has problems in fulfilling this aim. Female solidarity, or more simply the idea of girls together ... is an unambiguous sign of failure. (McRobbie, Angela, 1982, p. 282)

It encourages passivity:

> Romance is the language of passivity, *par excellence*. The romantic girl, in contrast to the sexual man, is *taken* in a kiss, or embrace. (ibid., p. 280)

It conceals frank discussion of female sexuality by euphemistically deploying the language of romantic love.

> It is about playing games which 'skirt about' sexuality, and which include sexual innuendo, but which are somehow 'nicer', 'cleaner' and less 'sordid'.... The girl's sexuality is understood and experienced not in terms of a physical need of her own body, but in terms of the romantic attachment. (ibid., p. 276)

What interests me looking down this list is that so much of what is identified as lacking in the girls' world of romance are features which are seen to be present in boys' books: the camaraderie (of the platoon, the gang); the explicit sexual activity (of *Lady Chatterley's Lover*?); the variety of social roles: 'Boys can *be* footballers, popstars, even juvenile delinquents, but girls can only be feminine' (ibid., p. 281). Such a view accepts at face value that boys' books cover a broad canvas and offer a multitude of different possibilities to their readers, whilst girls' books present only one small area: 'the narrow and restricted world of emotions' (ibid, p. 271).

How does this bear on my argument? I am about to turn to two more pieces of children's writing. The authors were in the same fourth-year English group as Angelique. One is a white girl, Joanna; the other a white boy, Stephen. Like Angelique's, their stories draw on popular fiction and, as one might predict, Stephen's story takes typically male themes – a fight and a bike chase – whilst Joanna's is a romance. Unlike Angelique's story, these texts seem at first glance completely conventional. My questions are: What happens in these texts? Does the fact that the writers have taken on board the conventions of their respective genres mean that they are locked into the world-view the genre proposes? And is this especially true of romance? What are the differences in the agendas they construct, the positions they offer for their male or female characters to speak from? Answering these questions is not going to be easy. I have already hinted above at some of the difficulties in reading romance. How can I avoid reading it only in terms of what it is not (male fiction) and construing what it is only in terms of a lack, a failure, an absence? Why not after all turn the contrast absence/presence on its head and consider male fiction as lacking the emotional depth, the complex exploration of personal relationships which the romance embodies? To move forward it seems to me that I must subject each text – the boy's and the girl's – to equal scrutiny. I cannot assume at the outset that I know what they will mean or how they mean it, that one is positive, the other negative, or view one only in the light of the other.

What follows is a reading of each text. These readings are personal, partial, incomplete. I have uncovered a variety of meanings crowding around the words in the texts, leading in different directions. I have not exhausted the work, nor provided the only way of seeing it, and

much of what I have said remains contradictory: an idea thrown up
at one point disappears elsewhere; alternative ways of reading the same
events remain unresolved. I am aware of gaps, times when I got stuck
twisting the material to yield up a particular view. Spotlighting one
feature of the text has meant excluding others. Another reader might
not make the same choices.

Despite all this seeming disorder the strategy I have adopted towards
Joanna's and Stephen's writing has a history. From reception theory
I have taken the idea that the text, rather than embodying a single
unitary meaning which the right reading will release, is open to
construction by the reader. That is to say, the text unread means
nothing. It is in the process of reading, through the interaction of
text and reader, that meaning is created. The reader's share in the
responsibility of meaning-making decentres the authority of the text.
In the process, a new question can be asked: What is it that the reader
brings to the text which makes meaning happen, renders the text
intelligible? In my readings, therefore, I have concentrated on what I
bring to the text.

From Barthes I have drawn on the distinction he makes in *S/Z*
between writerly and readerly texts. For Barthes, writerly texts force
attention on to their own construction by unsettling language and
breaking up the expected relation of signifier and signified; and they
do so by bringing into question the denotative role of the signifier.
Most texts do not fall into this category. They are readerly texts
which naturalise the process of their construction, making them seem
inevitable and therefore truthful. They seem to denote the very world
in which we live. Barthes goes on to argue that this is an illusion.
Rather than denoting something given, really out there, readerly texts
work by connotation: connotation which refers to other texts, other
bodies of social knowledge, other ways of seeing. They create the
illusion of the real by referring to other representations. In dealing
with Joanna's and Stephen's texts I have sought to unfold the ways
of seeing which underpin my readings and naturalise the text.

From Post-Structuralism I have taken the idea of the text's inherent
instability. The readerly text (to use Barthes's term) presents itself as
a homogeneous entity, coherent, whole. But it carries within itself the
seeds of its own destruction; to achieve unity it must continually
exclude, repress what it cannot own, and the mark of this act of

exclusion remains within the text. The repressed constantly returns, wriggling its way back on to the page. The text is riddled with contradiction rather than conformity. In my reading I have drawn attention to contradictions which surface and I have tried to show how the text attempts to conceal them.

I have not specifically mentioned Barthes's codes in the outline above, because I have not directly used them; that is, I have not systematised my reading and I did not start with them in mind as I did not want to pre-empt what I might find. Moreover, Barthes's categories draw fine distinctions which are not necessarily the ones I most want. Thus, for me, the distinction between expectations generated by social knowledge, or by knowledge of literary texts (genre), is important. Barthes collapses both together under the heading *cultural code*. I also need to define my notion of social knowledge more precisely. In part, it is generalised – how people of a certain kind behave – but in the context of these stories it is also particular: I know the writers personally, I know Thatch, so both texts also suggest their authors' presence. I hover therefore between the people these texts create and the authors themselves, who I know them as. The first text is written by Stephen. It is called 'It was time to leave'.

IT WAS TIME TO LEAVE

It started when I was riding round the streets on my Kwasaki 1300. I pulled up outside a pub. I removed my helmet and kept the engine ticking over. It was a hot sunny day.

There was a noise behind me. I looked round and saw two skin-heads. They were sloshed out of their minds and had probably been thrown out of the pub. One of them approched me stumbaling.

'Hey, Wherewolf' he said. At this he produced a flick knife and started to thrust it towards me. I picked up my helmet by the strap and swung it at his hand. I heard every little bone in his hand shatter as the helmet bounced off his hand. He let out a scream of pain and surprise. The knife fell to the grownd. He fell back onto the floor holding his hand.

Before I knew it his mate was on my back kicking, thumping, screaming and acting like a wild animal. I swung my helmet again, this time into his face. He stumbled on impact and fell to the ground unconcious.

With all the noise the other skin-heads in the pub started to pour out of the door. I took one look and pulled on the throttle. I burned away leaving the shouting skin-heads behind.

I was going about 90–95 miles per hour along the motorway, when a car came right up behind me and beeped its horn. I looked round and too my horror it was some of those skinheads so I excellerated more. The car drew up alongside me and one of the skinheads lent out of the window and said 'Want to learn to fly Wherewolf?'

He produced an iron bar which he thrusted towards my front wheel, I accelerated but he kept with me, so I put on the brakes. The car went zooming off. It did a hand break turn.

I turned off the motorway and got on a main road. I looked back. They were still following me.

I turned off the road and up an alley road. I thought I had lost them because they hadn't followed me up the alley.

As I pulled out the alley I heard screeching tyers it was those skinheads again. I started to accelerate faster and faster. The car that was now in front of me was slowing down. I had to overtake but there was a lorry coming the other way so I turned down to the left. I could see some traffic lights. They were green I had to make it. I passed through on Amber.

As I passed through an articulated lorry pulled out. I made it passed it but the car went straight under it and bursting into flames killing the skinheads.

I thought it was time to leave the scene so I headed for home.

*

It was time to leave.

What will precipitate this comment? Who will make the decision? The title acts as an invitation and sets up expectations. These questions will be answered, if I read on.

The story begins with the words 'It started when . . .' So the incident to be recounted has shape; it has a beginning – a point from which all subsequent action will flow – and by implication it will have an end: the moment of leaving. This suggests knowledge of a particular sort of story: rounded, (to be) complete. 'It started' – events will set in motion the process to be completed, and the narrator will take his/her place within them.

'I was riding around the streets on my Kwasaki 1300.' I know this piece was written by a boy, so I assume the narrator is male. There is nothing in the sentence to suggest otherwise, so I don't stop to think twice. But what sort of male? I hold two contrasting images. The motorbike is a 1300, an expensive machine, a powerful engine. The rider will be powerful too, able to control the machine, experienced, fearless, the hero of many adventures, Charles Bronson in leathers. Or perhaps a battle-scarred biker, proud of his skill, willing to test himself. In such a story there will be danger, perhaps violence.

But 'round the streets' pulls me another way, suggesting something much more homely: an aimless adolescent out on his bike, Stephen himself perhaps, going nowhere in particular, whiling away the hours before he has to be in. Behind the figure of a boy on a bike stands a whole network of classroom stories about teenage lives. Maybe this story is moving towards a chance encounter with a friend, an accident.

I pulled up outside a pub. I removed my helmet and kept the engine ticking over.

These next two sentences do nothing to resolve the question. Has he arrived to drink, or is the stopping place fortuitous? He does nothing except remove his helmet; the engine continues to run.

'It was a hot sunny day.' Has the narrator just noticed? Is he pausing in the heat? Or is this signalling the start of a different sort of story, which will tell of summer, lazing away the hours, taking things easy?

Looking at this first paragraph, what interests me is not so much the writer's apparently modern preoccupation with ambivalence and ambiguity – I'm not sure how much he was aware of this and I don't think it really matters whether he was or not – as how the text reveals itself as uncertain. It holds the seeds of several different stories, which could lead in different directions. It therefore offers up different possibilities, different spaces from which the narrator's identity can be construed. The same actions could mean different things, depending on how they are read, the context which places them. Yet the possibilities are not endless. What is holding (de)finite meanings at bay? And the reading depends more on my knowledge of masculinity, culled from other texts, other experiences, than on the words, devoid of association, which lie on the page.

There was a noise behind me. I looked around and saw two skin-heads.

The noise causes him to turn, to react. There are 'two skin-heads'. 'Skin-heads' instantly becomes read as male (why?) and speaks of a

particular sort of masculinity – young, hard, threatening, violent –
whose characteristics can be read through action: physically aggressive,
liable to fight. The word 'two' now takes on significance, counterposed
as it is to the narrator on his own. If there is to be a fight, he will be
at a disadvantage. But how will the skinheads react to the narrator?
This takes me back to the alternate images set up by the first paragraph.
They may read him as coolly impervious and therefore above their
notice, or as a potential target, someone whom they could pick off. So
around the question of who the narrator is, circles the question of
power. How much power does the narrator promise? Who is stronger
than whom? Who poses the greater threat?

> They were sloshed out of their minds and had probably been thrown out
> of the pub. One of them approached me stumbaling.

The skinheads are so drunk that they have 'probably been thrown out
of the pub'. Their drunkenness constitutes a threat, it is socially
unacceptable, it may lead to violence; at the same time it is proof of
their manhood, promising power. In leaving one group – the well-
behaved, the moderate – they have joined another – the hardened, the
defiant. *They* can drink this much and not be afraid of the consequences. 'Out of their minds' suggests they are beyond rational control.
'Stumbaling' draws attention to this, underlining a sense of the body
struggling to act on its own. Without the conscious mind, what is left
is their physical presence, the male body speaking of violence or
brutal sexuality. This is what makes me fear for the narrator, as the
adolescent, and hope that they are not coming for him, but simply
moving his way: 'approached'.

' "Hey, Wherewolf" he said.' Once the first word is spoken to the
narrator – 'Hey' – he is firmly placed as the object of the skinhead's
interest. To be noticed is to be challenged. This is the first move in
the encounter which will precipitate events for the rest of the story.
This is it. From now on the narrator will be caught up in the web of
others' actions, responding, reacting to what they have set in motion.
'Wherewolf' operates as the trigger, both as the insult, the label which
the narrator is dared to reject – 'You're ugly, you're a freak, I can
laugh at you' – and as the challenge, for it turns on its head the
assumptions about potential power and threat that the narrator had
been making about the skinheads. By calling him 'wherewolf' – the

man turned beast at the hour of midnight, predatory, violent, the source of death and destruction – they imbue him with the very violence he locates exclusively in them. Both constitute the other as the threat, the challenge is over who is more powerful; and the only way to settle this is to act it out, fight to decide. But in opening the challenge the skinheads are also assuming superiority. To take that risk is to dare to assume you can win.

Looking back now at the passage I have been working from, I am struck by its starkness. I have constructed a whole set of feelings in motion, yet Stephen's words speak only of actions. To work as a story it suggests the very thing it withholds. And there is something else. To maximise the threat the skinheads pose, I have read the narrator as a teenage boy, or at least kept in mind my uncertainties about who he is. I could read the curt tones of the text the other way: the authoritative, self-assured, powerful male, who observes the approach of his enemies with as much interest as he would a fly. I am not interested in resolving this question. I am drawing attention to the fact that both possibilities exist.

'At this he produced a flick knife . . .' The fight begins. The skinhead is carrying a knife. He is therefore prepared for violence. For him it may be the culmination of the day: go out, have fun, get drunk, get into a fight. Because the attacker is a skinhead, there is nothing special about the narrator as the object of aggression. He has done nothing to provoke an attack. The skinhead's violence, therefore, becomes random and vicarious.

By contrast, the narrator's weapon is what's nearest to hand – his helmet. Reason suggests that to respond with violence is his only way out. There is no sense of panic, no questioning: 'I picked up my helmet by the strap and swung it at his hand.' He is relying on his own physical resources, and this means his own physical strength. He has not gone looking for violence, but he can expect to react with it. In one sense, therefore, the skinhead and the narrator are utterly unlike in what they are seeking: it is the skinhead's commitment to violence which leads to an unprovoked attack. But they are also the same: they share the view that an encounter between men is a challenge over power and the means to resolve it is with physical aggression.

What do I make of 'I heard every little bone in his hand shatter'? The complete mastery of the narrator over his opponent? The utter

devastation of the attacker? And yet seeping through the lines there is
a sense of acute pain, the fragility of the aggressive fist. We move from
the sureness of the narrator's blow to the crumpling figure of the
skinhead, falling to the ground. The first sequence is completed.

> Before I knew it his mate was on my back, kicking, thumping, screaming
> and acting like a wild animal.

In place of the threatening, controlled playfulness of the opening move
by the first skinhead, the second skinhead is angry – angry and out of
control, reduced to a wild animal. His genuine feeling, anger, makes
him less deadly. In contrast, the narrator remains detached and determined: 'I swung my helmet again, this time into his face.' His blow
is cold and calculated, its effect related with scientific precision: 'He
stumbled on impact and fell to the ground unconcious.'

The second sequence ends like the first. The narrator emerges
unscathed, the winner:

> With all the noise the other skin-heads in the pub started to pour out of
> the door.

'Two skin-heads', 'his mate', 'the other skin-heads'. There is an
accumulating sense of threat here; the skinheads by their name are
part of a whole cultural grouping, a unified crowd who together
confront the narrator on his own. They will pursue the challenge.
Who the narrator is slips from sight as a question. It no longer matters.
He has been subsumed into a series of ritualised actions – of move,
counter-move, provocation, defence.

He has fought back and won. Now, to avoid defeat, he must escape.
Now that he has shown his strength, he can afford to show his
fear. For in the face of overwhelming odds flight becomes a
judicious retreat, fear common sense, and his leaving a display of
mastery:

> I took one look and pulled on the throttle. I burned away leaving the
> shouting skin-heads behind.

The scene now changes, and the second part of the story opens up:
The Chase. I've given the words initial capitals because it is a familiar
formula, especially from films. (In an interview I did with Stephen
about his writing he said that he'd taken the idea of trying to unseat

a bike rider by poking something in his wheels from a film he had seen.) Stephen re-creates the atmosphere of his model. The action is fast and furious as bike and car tear down the motorway and then into pursuit along busy town streets, up alleyways, losing and then finding each other, jostling for space on the roads with local traffic. His clauses become increasingly clipped as the tension mounts:

> I accelerated but he kept with me, so I put on the brakes. The car went zooming off. It did a hand break turn. I burned off the motorway and got on a main road. I looked back. They were still following me.

The narrator is the skilled bike rider using all his ingenuity and resources to manoeuvre his getaway, controling the power of the machine. Action dominates. Yet it is at precisely this moment in the text that uncertainties slip in. For the first time the narrator speaks of his own feelings: 'I looked round and too my horror it was some of those skinheads . . .'. His own grip on events is no longer certain:

> I thought I had lost them because they hadn't followed me up the alley.
>   As I pulled out of the alley I heard screeching tyres it was those skinheads again.

His competence is brought into question: 'I had to overtake . . . I had to make it.' The frightened adolescent resurfaces even at the moment of his greatest display of skill. The resolution of the chase comes with the utter obliteration of the skinheads. The story ends with an accident. The pursuing car crashes as the skinheads ignore a red light and collide with a lorry:

> The car went straight under it and bursting into flames killing the skinheads.

Their end has nothing to do with the narrator, because he has not engineered it. The blame for their death rests on themselves. They took too many risks, which ultimately they could not control. They must bear the consequences. Thus the spiral of violence is completed. At the end, as at the beginning, the narrator can sidestep any sense of involvement or responsibility. The violence which at the word 'Wherewolf' was momentarily shared by the narrator and the skinheads, which in the fight he showed himself as possessing, has been passed back to them and them alone. In The Chase he was fleeing, not fighting; he was escaping, seeking an end to the encounter.

They were provoking, trying to keep it alive. They did so not by appealing for revenge for their mates, defeated at the narrator's hands, but by returning to the playful, controlled, threatening sense of power they wield: '"Want to learn to fly Wherewolf?"' They do this because they are skinheads, and skinheads are violent by nature, the narrator is not. The narrator has detached himself from the encounter in which he has participated and can leave with a clear conscience: 'I thought it was time to leave the scene so I headed for home.'

The second text, written by Joanna, is called 'At the Party'.

AT THE PARTY

Lisa had spent all day in town trying to select something different to wear to the party tonight. She had ended up buying an all-in-one flying suit. She had picked the only blue one that was left in the shop, blue was her favourite colour.

Lisa, on the way home, stopped at Kingswood. She got off the bus and trudged onto the pavement. Lisa, who was weighed down with bags, slumped into the arcade. As soon as she was inside she set eyes on the boy she had fancied for ages.

'Hi Lisa, where have you been?' questioned Julie.

'In town' Lisa replied, not taking her eyes from her idol.

'You don't like Thatch again do you?' asked Julie.

'I might' Lisa answered. Lisa picked up her bags that were resting around her feet and walked towards Thatch.

'Alright Thatch, are you going to Cazzy's party tonight?' asked Lisa. She nearly fainted as he turned from his group of mates and gazed into her eyes.

'Pardon' asked Thatch.

Lisa's knees became weak, she felt herself going red so she looked down at the ground.

'Um, I just asked if you were going to Cazzy's party tonight'.

'Well I don't know, it depends if Mel is going. I asked her out last night' answered Thatch.

Lisa felt like crying, she didn't feel like going to the party anymore. Thatch walked away, so Lisa left to go home. She decided to go to the party after all, she was in the bathroom for over an hour, she soaked in the bath, cut her toenails, cleaned her teeth and put on her smelliest talcum powder, then into her new flying suit, she felt great, maybe there was no to luck with Thatch but there were plenty more boys going.

Lisa met her two friends before they went to the party. She didn't have to be in until twelve o'clock as long as somebody walked her home.

Lisa and her friends arrived at the party at eight o'clock. There was no sign of Thatch or Mel so Lisa sat down and helped herself to a drink. Some boy called Paul came over and started to chat her up. He asked her to go with him and she was just about to say yes as Thatch walked through the door without Mel!

'Um excuse me' said Lisa and pushed her way past Paul.

Lisa made her way out into the kitchen where Thatch was. Lisa couldn't see him in the kitchen and just as she was about to carry on searching two strong hands grabbed her around her waist. Lisa turned around to see Thatch's face only two inchs from hers. He slowly pulled her towards him and gave her a long, soft kiss. He slowly released his grip.

'Lisa I'm sorry. I just couldn't help myself. I finished with Mel after I had seen you. Will you go out with me?' asked Thatch.

Lisa looked at his handsome face, his dark ruffled hair gave a rebel effect. He look deep into her eyes. Lisa really loved him. She looked away.

'Well?' asked Thatch.

'Yes, I will go with you tonight' replied Lisa.

Thatch smiled, or was it more of a grin? He pulled Lisa towards him and kissed her again.

Lisa suddenly felt a sharp jab in her back.

'Right you cow get outside, I'm gonna do you in.'

Lisa turned around to see Mel stood there with tears in her eyes.

'Are you talking to me?' shouted Lisa angrilly.

'Yeah' replied Mel.

'Look you ugly dog, I was only seeing you for one night and now I like Lisa so ****! off' yelled Thatch.

Mel just stood there in shock her bottom lip began to quiver and then she bawled her eyes out.

'Thatch I HATE YOU' and with that Mel ran out the house slamming the door behind her.

'Lisa I really like you and there is no way that I'm gonna go with Mel again' whispered Thatch 'will you go out with me, please Lisa'.

Thatch looked into Lisa's eyes 'Please Lisa.'

'Yes' whispered Lisa 'I really like you'. [Thatch just please don't use me'.]

With that Lisa and Thatch kissed.

*

The title announces the setting and begins to suggest a focus for my attention. There will probably be a group of young people, boys and girls, having fun, away from adult supervision. There may be a romantic encounter. Any doubt as to what the story may contain is settled by the first paragraph. Lisa is choosing clothes for the party; ahead of her lies the chance of creating an impression (an impression for a boy) and the possibility of a romantic encounter. The careful choice of clothes speaks of the importance of appearance. What she wears, what she looks like, matters.

Yet how do I read this opening? It is difficult to be neutral about it. I can see it as already limiting the possibilities for action within the text. The girl's presence in the text is already fragmented, attention drawn to how she will look: by inference, how others will see her. She has to choose her clothes carefully, with others' eyes in mind.

> A woman must continually watch herself. She is almost continually accompanied by her own image of herself.... She has to survey everything she is and everything she does because how she appears to others, and ultimately how she appears to men, is of crucial importance for what is normally thought of as the success of her life. Her own sense of being in herself is supplanted by a sense of being appreciated as herself by another. (Berger, John, 1972, p. 46)

How can I write about Joanna's first paragraph? I can say that she is preoccupied now with trivia – her clothes – so that later she can be preoccupied with a boy, to whom her presentation of herself will signal her availability for romance. The trouble with such a reading is that behind it lies an assumption that she should be doing something else more important, more significant; and it smacks of contempt for the common preoccupation of young girls.

The alternative is to defend the paragraph to the hilt. After all, she chooses her flying-suit because it is *her* favourite colour, blue. She is taking pleasure in buying clothes for herself and does so on her own terms. Or look at the next paragraph, when she arrives at the arcade, trudging, slumping, 'weighed down with bags': the words telling their own tale, implicitly criticising the image of carefree teenage consumerism.

I am caught between two images: the teenage girl sucked in by sexist ideology, completely dominated by its reference points; or the teenage girl rightfully pursuing her own interest, realistically appraising what she's taken on board. One approach seems too negative, the second impossible to maintain. Either way, whether I attack or condone it, Joanna's writing begins its reading as a potential source of blame. Women are the foolish sex. This is the unspoken charge I must answer.

It is hard to avoid taking up a defensive stance. How can I extricate myself and the text from these bleak alternatives? Try this. Turn the protagonist of the story from Lisa to Len, turn the pronouns from she to he, now read the first paragraph again. The prose settles back down into a neutral space. Actually, not much is going on in this paragraph. Clothes are being bought in a fairly desultory sort of way, a certain amount of information is being given (there is a party tonight, the protagonist's favourite colour is blue). One could safely assume that the writer is doing what most writers do: slowly winding herself up before getting on to the interesting bits. Parties are preceded by clothes-buying; when buying clothes the colour does matter, so jot that down and the story has begun. It's setting the scene.

Before I go any further with my reading I want to stop a minute to think about what has been going on in my last few paragraphs. In writing about Stephen's piece I became increasingly aware of how much I brought to my reading. Meanings clustered around the words in the text, inviting inclusion. I got most profit from that reading not by seeking for a single unitary theme but by pointing to the traces of different, often opposed meanings dispersed through the text, surfacing at one moment and then disappearing to re-emerge later. I did not begin by consciously looking for such contradictions. (My earliest glance at the piece had left me with the impression of the narrator as lone hero, fighting fearlessly through numerous obstacles to final success.) I began simply by writing down whatever came to mind and then seeing what happened. Reading Joanna's piece I am aware that I have begun embattled, hemmed in. It has taken me several paragraphs to argue through the various approaches I could take and arrive at the conclusion that there's not much going on at the beginning of her piece. Before I say anything I have had consciously to clear the decks in a way I didn't have to for Stephen. To extricate Joanna's text from a debate about the nature of femininity, the value of female activity, requires hard work, such is the cultural luggage I bring with me to my reading. Stephen's piece – male writing – does not generate such activity.

Back to Joanna's writing. Things really pick up and start happening when Lisa reaches the arcade. After the prologue, the first scene:

> As soon as she was inside she set eyes on the boy she had fancied for ages.

Who the boy is is unimportant. He simply acts as a focal point for Lisa's feelings. We don't need to know anything else about him. The information that she had fancied him for ages implies that so far there has been no relationship between them. He has been observed from a distance, the object of her desire, a desire as yet unspoken. It doesn't matter, for here feelings precede action. They do not need explanation. They hold a promise for what might happen in the future. This story will explore that promise.

Lisa's friend cuts in on her thoughts: ' "Hi, Lisa, where have you been?" questioned Julie.' Julie remains disembodied, a voice which Lisa hears whilst her eyes remain fixed on the boy. ' "In town" Lisa replied, not taking her eyes from her idol.' The other girl cannot pierce Lisa's absorption in her own feelings. Once again it is the feelings themselves which seem important. The boy is her idol, like a pop-star up on stage, a million miles from the worshipping crowd. The distance between her and him does not matter, so long as she can gaze.

> 'You don't like Thatch again do you?' asked Julie.
> 'I might' Lisa answered.

Julie is not asking Lisa about what she intends to do, what she is up to – she wants to know what Lisa is feeling. The reader already knows the answer to this question, but Lisa's answer to Julie is ambiguous: 'I might'. Feelings are private, not to be made public. Lisa's feelings absorb her, cutting her off from Julie. For Julie, the question ' "You don't like Thatch again do you?" ' is about return of a feeling – a feeling which leads where? But for Lisa, who had fancied the boy for ages, the expression of feeling is about continuity – her feeling is constant, central to the way she is (acting).

The word idol suggests pop magazines and pin-ups – the cool young faces staring out silently from the pages, images which become the focus for powerful emotions. But powerful in what way? Over-whelming – of self, meaning surrender, submission; or of others, implying engulfing, consuming, snaring? (Who speaks these words, offers these alternatives? Whom do they construct as the possessor of strong feelings?) But the boy idol is also named – Thatch. I know him. He exists. He left in the fifth year, the year before I taught Joanna. Fantasy and reality trip each other up.

In the few lines that I have been looking at, Joanna has not gone beyond naming Lisa's feeling – 'fancied'. That is the resting point, the explanation of her behaviour. When the story goes on,

> Lisa picked up her bags that were resting around her feet and walked towards Thatch.

my view of what she does is coloured by my knowledge of her feelings. I imagine her overwhelmed by her sense of his presence, moving towards him as if in a dream. He becomes the source of feelings *which were her own*. As with Stephen's piece, and violence, so in this too the responsibility, the ownership of feelings becomes something uncertain. Stephen's piece offered me the skinheads as the location of the violence. Joanna's piece offers me Thatch as the location of desire, desire which began with her. Because I can understand Lisa's actions as arising from her feelings, and her feelings have their source not in herself but in Thatch, in watching her move across the floor towards him it is as if he is pulling her. Her actions are no longer her own. They disappear as the object of my study. How can I retrieve them, give them back to her?

Again, if I switch the genders round, turn the dialogue between Julie and Lisa into Joe and Len and then read through the passage down to ' "Alright Thatch, are you going to Cazzy's party tonight?" ' the whole encounter re-forms itself. L (Len/Lisa)'s actions become foregrounded, speaking louder than words. L (Len/Lisa) pays little attention to the conversation, because s/he is about to act. Moving across the floor becomes purposefully stalking his/her prey and the opening remarks to Thatch become a straight pick-up, carrying with it all the assurance of success. My attention strays no futher than to what s/he is doing.

What I am pointing out by doing this is that the same words on the page mean something very different, depending on the context within

which I read them (masculinity/femininity). In other words, I bring
to the text assumptions about gender which inevitably channel the
way I read. Reading the passage with a girl in mind I have emphasised
emotion, and doing this when the emotion can be seen as in some
sense Thatch's (he is its source; without him it wouldn't exist) I
denude the girl's action of purpose. It becomes symbolic, not the
source of meaning in itself but revealing something other than itself,
something behind it (feelings). To read in this way, what position do
I take up? Reading the passage with a boy in mind the action stands
alone, decisive. My reading fragments Lisa's presence. Once again I
find myself hemmed in.

What does the text itself have to say about Lisa's action? She makes
her move boldly, singling out Thatch from his mates – 'group of
mates'. This is not a gaggle of girls waiting to be broken up by a boy's
presence, from whom a girl will turn eagerly, but a crowd of boys,
self-absorbed, reluctant to give way to a girl. Because she is a girl the
boldness of her approach: ' "Alright Thatch, are you going to Cazzy's
party tonight?" ' has already been undercut by hesitancy. Her action
is a cover for, speaks of her powerful emotions. And these emotions
keep on threatening to break through: 'She nearly fainted. . .'. Now it
is Thatch's turn to act. Lisa has made the opening move. In return:

> he turned from his group of mates and gazed into her eyes.
> 'Pardon?' asked Thatch.

How do I read his response? He gazes into her eyes as she had gazed
at him? A sign of longing, submission, an act of intimacy? This reading
is countered by 'Pardon?'. Deference to her, or indifference? Because
he does not recognise the specialness of this moment for her, what
could be a private, meaningful exchange is transformed into a public
encounter. She reacts with confusion and embarrassment:

> Lisa's knees became weak, she felt herself going red so she looked down
> at the ground.

How can she react to him? To challenge his lack of interest would be
to give herself away, make herself vulnerable by revealing her true
feelings, feelings which are private, which her body threatens to betray:
'she felt herself going red . . .'. In an effort to be casual her voice
communicates hesitancy: ' "Um, I just asked if you were going to

Cazzy's party tonight".' Her attention to him led her to speak; his indifference to her switches her attention back on herself – a self awkward and uncomfortable. She must control her outward display:

> 'Well I don't know, it depends if Mel is going. I asked her out last night' answered Thatch.

Thatch is unavailable for romance, he has another girl. This is the significance of his remarks for Lisa. Has he recognised that she was asking him out, probing the possibility of romance? Is he being callous, or blithely casual, because he is simply unaware?

I am watching Thatch through Lisa's eyes, a girl looking at a boy. In her text I have seen the contrast between them as drawn in terms of power. He has the power to make her happy if he will recognise and return her emotions. He remains powerful in this encounter because he is unmoved. Disclosing what she feels will make her powerless; struggling to control her emotions makes her seem weak. He is in control of his emotions, she is not. Yet if the relationship is to happen he must lose that control. The struggle is to be able to be weak, to give in to deep feeling. That means finding a private space where vulnerability can be shared. Here she has to play the public encounter by the rules of control, hiding what she is feeling, whilst inside: 'Lisa felt like crying, she didn't feel like going to the party anymore.' The text depicts a world of tension and disparity, where what she feels cannot be clearly spoken, given public voice.

'She decided to go to the party after all, she was in the bathroom for over an hour.' A list of what she does follows. The simplicity of the description reminds me of the first paragraph. Both show Lisa on her own: self-contained, uncomplicated. For the first time action precedes and creates feeling.

> She soaked in the bath, cut her toenails, cleaned her teeth and put on her smelliest talcum powder, then into her new flying suit, she felt great.

Dealing with others means preparing to shift ground, being hard to pin down. On her own she stands for herself, not a veiled meaning. I, the reader, share her knowledge of herself alone, a shared private knowledge, which reveals the public disguise. 'Maybe there was no to luck with Thatch but there were plenty more boys going.' Is it a statement of purpose, undercutting Thatch's value, showing that it is not so much him she wants as the chance to be in love, enjoy her feelings to the full, without public constraint? Or does it suggest that the successful outcome of partying depends on the prospect of meeting boys, becoming the object of their desire as Thatch was the object of hers? That she can effect this only by signalling her availability for pleasure through her appearance? That she has no control over who will take up the promise?

> Lisa met her two friends before they went to the party. She didn't have
> to be in until twelve o'clock as long as somebody walked her home.

Her presence at the party is dependent on adult consent, adult regulation of her behaviour and concern for her safety: 'as long as someone walked her home'. Being out on the street alone late at night spells danger and vulnerability.

When she arrives at the party: 'There was no sign of Thatch or Mel...'. The first encounter with Thatch ended in disappointment, but Lisa is still thinking about him. There may be another encounter. Will she manage to claim Thatch? To claim him will also be to disinherit Mel.

'Some boy called Paul came over and started to chat her up.' Paul is only 'some boy'; he lacks the significance of Thatch because she has no special feeling for him, so the ritual chatting-up becomes empty – a business contract. She can weigh it up, assess the pros and cons, make a cool decision. She is detached. And Paul? Because he is a boy I assume he is not signalling his availability for romance so much as assessing hers. He will ask the questions, judge the response, decide whether to ask her out. She waits, and answers. He is confident, powerful, a smooth operator. I know what he does, his actions speak for themselves, I view him through the girl's eyes: he assumes she is available for him if only she will say yes. I contrast his directness – it is obvious what he is doing – with her hesitancy in approaching Thatch. She has to conceal, disguise what she is doing, keep in check the emotions which threaten to overwhelm her, whilst he can be open, self-assured (because he is indifferent? any girl will do, will signal his status to the other boys as powerful male, possessor of a girl?). To the boy (Paul or Thatch) the narrative gives no space for feelings. He becomes what she is not.

Yet it is Lisa who closes the encounter by behaving with abrupt indifference: ' "Um excuse me" said Lisa and pushed her way past Paul.' She has noticed Thatch, Thatch who is the site of her desire, a desire which by its presence transforms the contract between girls and boys (going out) into romance.

I wonder about the boys' presence in this piece. I am drawn to see them through Lisa's eyes, through my own eyes, as a woman. I interpret their behaviour, construct them as cool, powerful, able to choose (unlike Lisa, who is driven by her strong feelings, compelled to act). They remain aloof, even indifferent. Constructed in this way, what is it I feel for them – envy, annoyance, contempt? Contempt resurfaces. Again I find myself taking sides. What is excluded from this picture? Their anxiety, their own sense of hesitation, nervousness about coming forward, making the first move towards the girl? I see their interest in the girl as part of their self-interest, in possessing her. I imagine them as playing a game. I do not construct Lisa in this way. Yet I could. Such a reading is available – Lisa as manipulative, setting them up, playing for control, playing for power. A male reading of Lisa's actions. And she is as indifferent and callous towards Paul as Thatch had seemed towards her. I justify her actions because she is in love, condemn theirs because I assume they are not. They are exercising choice. She is driven by desire.

In the next sequence Lisa is looking for Thatch in the kitchen. Suddenly

> two strong hands grabbed her around her waist. Lisa turned around to see Thatch's face only two inches from her. He slowly pulled her towards him and gave her a long, soft kiss. He slowly released his grip.

Her desire is fulfilled because he desires her. The longing is over. He does what she wants to do/be done. At the same time, because it is he alone who acts she is not responsible for the nature of their encounter. She has precipitated it by looking for him, but at the moment when they meet she does nothing. It is his sexuality which claims my attention, not hers. Her sexuality remains outside the text, unspoken of. But what would it mean to acknowledge it when female sexual assertiveness labels a girl a slag? Because I know nothing of his feelings I can also read his actions as exercising mastery: he is controlling her, claiming power. He has the girl. Once again I see his actions as powerful, hers as given over to power. A girl making the same approach as Thatch's would be read as overwhelmed by passion. What stops me making this same interpretation of Thatch?

Thatch kissing Lisa could be the moment of closure, the moment at which the story ends, romance starts. But for Lisa to be safe (from what?) the uncertainties which surround Thatch's actions must be resolved. Is he a predatory male out for what he can get, giving nothing of himself in return, seeking only physical pleasure, who will exploit Lisa's openness to his advances, of whom she should beware? Or are his actions safe because they spring from deep feeling; he will also take care of her?

> 'Lisa I'm sorry. I just couldn't help myself. I finished with Mel after I had seen you. Will you go with me?' asked Thatch.

He apologises for his behaviour. Why? Is it out of place, has he overstepped his mark? In what way? By revealing his inner feelings, or his sexuality? His sexuality could be a source of power for him, degrading of her. He is nervous of her response, a response I am sure of. He has done what she wants. He has selected her. The boy whom she had fancied for ages has returned her desire. In so doing he raises questions about what sort of desire she holds for him – innocent or sexual. How could her desire be innocently devoid of sexuality in an encounter where adolescent boy meets girl? Her sexuality is placed by romance, love, the power of feelings: his sexuality by physical presence, the power of the body. And in this text? Where is he speaking from? I am uncertain.

> Lisa looked at his handsome face, his dark ruffled hair gave a rebel effect. He look deep into her eyes.

In answer to his question Lisa looks at him, appraising his appearance, just as earlier she had concentrated on her own. She studies the surface image, whilst he gazes deep into her eyes. She seems detached and careful, whilst his look suggests intimacy, longing.

> Lisa really loved him.

What does this sentence mean? It offers a summary of what is going on and by its completeness threatens to bring my questioning to an end. I need look no further to understand. In a romance this is the reason girls behave as they do. Love covers over questions of sexuality, wiping them from view. Yet the sentence seems misplaced, occurring as it does in the middle, not at the end, of the negotiations between Thatch and Lisa about the nature of the contract they are entering into – negotiations where sex, power, vulnerability, private feelings, public space jostle each other as they chase across the page. 'She really loved him' cannot stop the movement.

> She looked away.
> 'Well?' asked Thatch.
> 'Yes, I will go with you tonight' replied Lisa.

She is cautious. She does not reveal her feelings to him. Her answer is precise, her response cool in the face of his pleading. 'Thatch smiled, or was it more of a grin?' The ambivalence of the text, my inability to decide who is vulnerable, who holds power and is in control, surfaces directly here. If he smiles, then he signals relief from his own uncertainty, vulnerability; he is warm and relaxed, open to tender feelings. If he grins, then he signals distance, knowing control; he holds the power, possesses her. 'He pulled Lisa towards him and kissed her again.' He has been asking her, waiting for her reply. Now he once again takes the initiative. Thatch has made his choice, Lisa has agreed to be chosen.

What about Mel? ' "Right you cow get outside, I'm gonna do you in." ' To be secure in her possession of Thatch, Lisa's rival – Mel – must be defeated. The fact that she contests Lisa's possession of Thatch shows his value. Her challenge, angry and full of hurt, shows the price that Lisa must pay. She has won Thatch on her own at the cost of excluding all others, disregarding their feelings. But there is another reading to be made. If Thatch is honest, his professions of love trustworthy, he must make it clear that he exists for Lisa alone. His commitment to her must be serious enough to exclude the possibility of him seeing other girls, playing them off against each other, and in the process maintaining his own power. He too must become vulnerable. Mel begins by attacking Lisa. It is Thatch who settles the contest:

> 'Look you ugly dog, I was only seeing you for one night and now I like Lisa so **** off!' yelled Thatch.

His commitment to Lisa here is clear, but he reduces Mel to tears and rage! At the moment when Lisa's possession of him seems most secure he also reveals himself as hurtful and indifferent to the pain he causes. My uncertainty about his actions remains.

Thatch has controlled the conflict between Mel and Lisa and brought it to an abrupt end. In a businesslike voice he summarises his position:

> 'Lisa I really like you and there is no way that I'm gonna go with Mel again' ...

But once again he suddenly seems to relinquish power: '... whispered Thatch 'will you go out with me, please Lisa''. Lisa agrees: '"Yes" whispered Lisa "I really like you."' The contract is sealed. He has established honourable terms. He won't two-time her, he will be loyal, love will grow. But the penultimate sentence in the story has been crossed out. It reads 'Thatch just please don't use me.' Like me, Lisa/Joanna can't make up her mind about Thatch.

6

Writing: The Struggle over Meaning

As we've seen, teachers use the word 'derivative' to dismiss writing they do not like and cannot approve of, whether from a Leavisite, Media Studies or anti-sexist perspective. The word is used selectively in relation to a particular body of texts: broadly, those which reproduce the central features of popular fiction. Inevitably, its use is therefore bound up with particular systems of values, whether moral, aesthetic or political. Moreover, teachers working within a Leavisite, Media Studies or anti-sexist perspective are concerned that in reproducing a form of which they disapprove children are also endorsing a set of values which teachers don't like. This turns the writers of such fictions into at best hapless victims of a powerful ideology they cannot contest, or at worst into active co-conspirators with a set of values which works against their own long-term best interests. But by taking a different approach to how I read conventional texts, as I did in the last chapter, some new questions have emerged. Joanna's and Stephen's texts seem much less certain, much less closed than I initially thought, for all that they reproduce many of the familiar features of popular fiction. I need to give a new account of what is going on here and, in particular, of what happens when writers reproduce elements of other texts in their own.

Let me begin by briefly digressing into the field of linguistics: to the attack on the behavioural model of language acquisition made by Chomsky and subsequently by others using the work of Vygotsky. Chomsky took issue with the behaviourists, whose theory of language acquisition was one of imitation reinforced by reward. For the behaviourists, the child (and would-be speaker) learns language by listening, internalising and then reproducing the sounds heard. If she does so correctly she is rewarded, presumably because the message is understood, wishes can be carried out, contact can be made. The reward reinforces what has been learnt. According to this view, there-fore, the child is a *tabula rasa* upon which sounds are imprinted, to be stored and then simply reproduced. Chomsky attacked this model of child as machine, unengaged with what is taking place, except in the most mechanical way, and replaced it with a view of children as active, creative, thinking human beings, forming hypotheses about language on the basis of what is heard and thus formulating rules for their own language use. In this way he could account for the fact that speakers of a language can utter sentences they themselves have never heard, and children in the process of learning that language can, by overgeneralising from the rules, produce forms that adult speakers never use. For Chomsky, to learn a language is, therefore, to acquire the ability to manipulate it, rather than only to submit to what is already there.

I want to concentrate on this move from child as passively taught to child as active learner within the context of educational theory and particularly in relation to the work of Vygotsky. I am turning to Vygotsky for two reasons. First, because Chomsky's usefulness in attacking behaviourism has been somewhat undercut by the fact that he went on to explain the complexity of language acquisition by posing an innate human capacity, the Language Acquisition Device. As John Searle has shown (Searle, John, 1972, pp. 16–24), this position takes him dangerously close to the empiricist theories he so convincingly demolished. Second, because Vygotsky does more than set an active learner at the centre of his theory. He also puts forward a complex account of the dialectal relationship between children's development and their sociocultural and material environment as he describes the learning process. In Vygotsky's description children are born into a social world where language already exists, shaped by culture and history. When they come to take over its words they have to struggle intellectually to take over its meanings. Word meanings do not come complete. They evolve for children as they try them out within specific cultural contexts. The process of acquiring language is thus a process of active internalisation, which then continuously reacts back on the environment.

I am proposing that a similar process is at work with respect to reading and writing, that what holds good for language acquisition as a whole is also true for other language practices besides speech. In other words, if children's writing shows the traces of other texts, then those texts have been actively reconstituted there, and it is out of that process of reconstitution that meaning arises. Meaning is not absolutely predetermined – written in tablets of stone, as it were, and fixed for all eternity outside any one text. It is continuously open to change as it is re-established here and now. If I accept this view it becomes meaningless to look for signs of empty reproduction as proof of passive acceptance of the reproduced. Moreover, it also rids me of the proposition underlying much of the argument about popular culture: that children learn directly through passive imitation. The argument voiced within Media Studies, the Leavisite tradition and anti-sexism, in so far as it posits passive consumers of popular fiction, is at heart a behaviourist one.

If meaning has to be re-established in any one context, I do not consider that the rehearsal of a particular form brings with it for the writer a firm grasp or the outright acceptance of a particular set of values. Writing alone does not shape what we think. We bring what we know to the text and try to push it into shape. The act of writing continually threatens to dissolve what we know, even as it promises to finalise it and pin it down. What we think is always threatening to break out from the form which would constrain it, precisely because the form itself continually evokes other forms which it is not: one word, one phrase can set off a whole new train of associations and turn the text in a new direction.

A good example of what I mean here is given by Angelique's story 'Again!'. Of the three texts I have commented on this is probably the easiest for teachers to approve of, because the ending is so clearly oppositional and invokes a set of values that many teachers would want to endorse: strong girls, loyal to female friends and distrustful of boys. But in terms of technique it is in many ways the weakest of the three: the tone is uneven, and the text at times awkward or even incoherent. The final part of the story, where Paul's attitude towards Clare leads the narrator to end her relationship with him, is particularly muddled. The phrases used to describe the action unsettle the smooth unfolding of events precisely because they so strongly evoke another sort of ending, which the author clearly doesn't want here: one where the boy deserts a helpless girl. Now my argument in relation to that text was that its very incoherence was also its strength. Angelique's text is successful precisely because it is able to exploit the disparity between different ways of reading events that her words evoke. In the process a new sort of story is created – one which allows the author to make her own point: 'I want everyone to know that if I have a boyfriend, my boyfriend ain't going to hit me about, if anything I'm going to hit him about.'

Angelique is quite clear about the purpose of her own writing. In this I suspect she is probably unusual. Certainly, the other children I have spoken to are not so clear about what they want to say when they put pen to paper, and indeed many are mainly committed to finishing the task as quickly and easily as possible. After all, they are generally writing for homework or in class and under the teacher's directions. But that does not mean that they don't face the same sort of difficulties in sticking to the main line of their story and creating a uniform and homogeneous text. Indeed, one of the reasons teachers are able to hold up unity and coherence of style as major criteria of excellence is precisely because most children don't achieve it. Far from being trapped by the boundaries of any one genre, most children struggle to hold divergent sets of material together.

The soap opera I quoted from at the beginning of Chapter 2 shows this quite clearly. The author has used her understanding of soap opera to shape each chapter of her work into the equivalent of one television episode. Each chapter has at least one dramatic moment. There is a large cast of characters, brought together in one place, and various plots are intertwined. Each chapter ends on a cliffhanger. But at the same time the writer has chosen Cambridge University as her setting and made the characters medical students. This brings with it other expectations about how the people in her story will behave. For the teacher who marked the work it is the author's failure to understand or use the conventions associated with Cambridge and middle-class intellectual life which spoils the story. For the author her ignorance of this set of conventions is supplemented by other sorts of knowledge. Her portrait of university life is partly predicated on school life. There are some obvious continuities: bells ring at the end of lessons, there is break-time, tutors are called teachers. There are also some differences: teachers give individual students lessons (not tutorials or seminars).

At the same time power relations between students and teachers are modified so that students can get drunk with their teachers or have affairs. A key plot development is the affair between Andrew and Ms Rabbit, who gets pregnant. Various pieces of information about Cambridge complete the picture; for example, that students use bicycles as their main means of getting from place to place. Bicycles feature prominently in at least two incidents which are central to the plot. Punting is also mentioned and provides the dramatic backdrop for some of the action.

When it comes to writing about the relationship between her male and female characters, the author draws again on her knowledge of soap operas to establish some melodramatic plot lines: pregnancy and possible abortion, malicious interference with the course of true love and dramatic quarrels. But her interpretation of character is also dependent on what she knows about how people of her own age behave. Charles's attempt to persuade Joe to share rooms with him takes place at a time when they seem to be doing homework together, and is brought to an end by Joe insisting that he stop pestering her so that she can get on with her work:

> Charles and Joe were sitting down and doing work.
>   'Joe'
>   'Yes Charles'
>   'How would you like to share rooms'
>   'Charles, I don't know I'll think about it'
>   'Oh go on' said Charles
>   'If you really want me to tell you, no I don't want to share rooms, as you can see I have a lot of work to do'
>   'OK, OK'
> and they both changed the subject and started talking about the weather.

The soap–opera genre may be the dominant influence on this piece of work, but it is supplemented by other divergent sorts of information coming from different and often contradictory contexts.

So my argument is that children have to struggle to rehearse a particular genre. Language itself is sufficiently unstable to make that task hard, whilst each genre is always transected by other sets of knowledge, whether of other genres, other texts children have read or other stories they can tell about their own lives. It is precisely this propensity of language to refer onwards to other contexts in which it is deployed – contexts which are contradictory, not uniform – that I have exploited in my analysis of the stories written by Angelique, Stephen and Joanna. What we think, what we know, the contexts we can refer to, are all shaped by language, which is itself part and parcel of social practices. By drawing attention to its diversity and instability I am suggesting that language both maps on to existing social contexts and also has the potential to reconfigure them.

Up to this point I have been stressing the way in which the boundaries of any one genre can be transected in children's writing by references to other sets of knowledge, yet despite this pressure each genre is also potentially self-contained and coherent. So in taking up one particular genre children are making a choice. Each genre is distinguishable by virtue of its own history, both in terms of who produces it and who reads it and, most importantly, what it establishes as its own focus of interest. Most of us would find little difficulty in recognising the following minimal definitions:

> The central fantasy of the adventure story is that of the hero – individual or group – overcoming obstacles and dangers and accomplishing some important and moral mission. (Cawelti, John, 1976, p. 39)

> The crucial defining characteristic of romance is not that it stars a female but that its organizing action is the development of a love relationship, usually between a man and a woman. (ibid., p. 41)

> The fundamental principle of the mystery story is the investigation and discovery of hidden secrets, the discovery usually leading to some benefit for the character(s) with whom the reader identifies. (ibid., p. 43)

So what happens when children seek to work within the boundaries of one particular genre, and what governs that choice? Let me return to Joanna's and Stephen's texts.

The first comment I want to make – again, but with a difference in the light of my new position – is that their choice of genre is gender-specific. That is to say, the adventure story, encompassing retributive violence dealt out by the good guys to the bad, is a familiar theme in comics aimed at boys. The romance in which the girl pursues and gets her man is a familiar theme in magazines aimed at girls. From my own classroom observation I would say that teenage boys frequently take up the adventure theme in their writing, teenage girls the romance, but that it is rare for girls to write adventure stories centring round male heroes battling against innumerable odds and practically unheard of for boys to write romances. (I did once set this whole class a romance title: 'She walked away without saying goodbye'. Most of the boys avoided doing the homework by simply failing to hand their books in. Only one of them really tried to explore a relationship with a girlfriend; Stephen turned his story into an encounter with a traffic warden who'd given him a parking ticket – and it wasn't romantic!)

Let me think about these gender-specific genres a little further. The adventure story of the kind I've outlined, played out in boys' comics, rarely includes female characters. Men are judged against other men. The question posed is about who is most powerful, and the solution to this dilemma is sought most frequently through a display of physical strength. The romance played out in girls' comics encompasses both male and female characters. Starting from a position of distance (the girl desires a relationship with the boy), it moves towards closeness. The dilemmas which must be negotiated are: will the boy approve of the girl, can the girl safely approve of the boy? The solution thus depends upon the possibility of successful interpretation of behaviour.

Why should teenage boys and girls continually return to such gender-specific genres? My answer is that such genres offer places from which to explore gender identity. The boys' adventure story proposes masculinity as its focal point – what being a man might mean. The girls' romance proposes feminity understood in its relation to masculinity – what the encounter between the two might mean. Given that I have rejected the notion that boys and girls passively learn either gender roles or anything else from their readings of popular fiction, what am I talking about when I say 'explore gender identity'? How could that mean anything except reduplicating well-worn positions? I have placed at the heart of my view of writing an active writer engaged in reworking the material they start with, material which is itself diverse rather than uniform. The genre pre-exists the writer, just as language pre-exists the speaker. The writer refashions the genre in the process of using it, making it fit the present sphere of action. Each genre is not itself a homogeneous entity. It is made up of bits and pieces which must be dismantled, parts forgotten or excluded, reshaped, put back together differently, to fit the particular story the

writer is working on. It must be tugged into place, its meaning re-
established here. As such it will always be open to manipulation,
exploration.

There is one further point to be stressed: Vygotsky reminds us that
such a process (the tussle over appropriation of meaning) always takes
place within a particular cultural environment. Vygotsky's account of
play, which he saw as prefiguring writing, is of particular relevance
here:

> In one sense a child at play is free to determine his own actions, but in
> another sense this is an illusory freedom, for his actions are in fact
> subordinated to the meaning of things and he acts accordingly. (Vygotsky,
> Lev, 1978, p. 103)

The work that goes on in writing does not happen in a vacuum, but
refers outwards to 'the meaning of things': the socially constructed
world. So my view of Joanna's and Stephen's texts is that they reveal
the writers in the process of exploration, struggling over meaning both
within the text and as it is socially constituted. To substantiate this
claim I want to draw together some of the threads in my own reading.
I shall begin with Stephen's text.

The story begins by delineating images of maleness: there is my
query over the presence of the narrator – aimless adolescent prey to
an aggressive male challenge, or self-assured adult confident in his
claim to power? Against the narrator stand the skinheads. Named by
their physical appearance, 'out of their minds' with drink, they are a
reminder of the violent physical power of the male body. These are
potentially negative qualities, and within this story the skinheads are
quickly established as the bad guys whose threat must be taken up
and defeated. But physical power is also a necessary attribute of
manhood. To be a man is to have the ability not to be afraid, to be
prepared to respond with physical violence and to do so accurately
and with skill. So on the one hand the text must divide up absolutely
the good guys from the bad guys to ensure that the bad guys receive
their just deserts whilst the good guys escape unharmed. On the other
the text is confronted with the knowledge that in order to win the
good guys must manifest the same characteristics as the bad guys, so
what is the difference? What I am suggesting here is that the images
of masculinity on which Stephen draws are not hard and fast, but

fragile constructions liable to collapse into each other at any moment.

Another feature of the text which interests me is the displacement of feelings. To wield male power successfully, action must dominate. (The skinhead who attacks in anger does so ineffectually.) No mention is made of the narrator's state of mind until over halfway through, yet the story works precisely because it re-creates tension and makes me fear for the narrator's successful escape unscathed. It is a double movement, both away from and towards what would be repressed. Again I am drawn to the narrowness of the line Stephen must tread.

In making these comments I am not trying to point out curious features of the text as they lie on the page but to suggest that they mark social dilemmas which the author must negotiate. Let me once again pick out the bare bones of the story. It is about a violent attack made by skinheads (male) on the narrator, because he is also male. It is about the possibility of escaping and ending that challenge. It is about blame for the way things began, responsibility for the way they turn out. It addresses itself to problems which are a social reality: what masculinity signifies, what it might mean thus to be read as male. The struggle for power between men is both at the centre of the genre which Stephen employs and at the centre of the many stories boys tell about their own lives. I am reminded of the many classroom stories of violence up at Kingswood at the weekend and in particular of the boys' fear of that violence. The stories were less about active participation in violent events than about escape from situations which looked as if they might offer violence: running home alone in the dark, afraid of being jumped. It was the boys who walked the streets at night in fear!

Yet in addressing these dilemmas, the narrator in Stephen's text doesn't simply fit into a given unitary role and solve the problem by the straightforward assumption of power. On the contrary, behind the figure of the assertive and powerful male lurks the frightened adolescent peeping between the lines. To avoid being labelled a coward the narrator must participate in the violence of the first attack. To emerge without blame he must not be seen as its source. To be picked on he has to be potentially weak; to survive he has to be strong. To flee he has to exercise common sense and skill; to do so too soon would be to exhibit too much fear, to do so too late, too much bravado. The text is a piece of delicate negotiation about masculinity as it is socially constituted and Stephen's possible place within that reading.

What about Joanna's text? If Stephen's text raises questions about acting as a male in a world where masculinity can be challenged by other men, Joanna's raises questions about acting as a female in a world defined by male power. In her story Lisa seeks a relationship with Thatch. The encounter between the two of them begins with a statement of Lisa's feelings. The difficulty the story poses is how those feelings can be fulfilled (will Lisa get together with Thatch?). The text centres around problems of signification and interpretation of female behaviour in a particular patriarchal cultural setting. I say this because so much of what Joanna dwells on is to do with how the boy (constructed as holding the power) will perceive the girl. Will Lisa's first move towards Thatch make her seem too strident, challenging his power? Will it make her own feelings obvious? The text, by documenting the girl's attempts at awkward concealment, suggests the necessity for disguise, an understanding that making her feelings known to Thatch before she is sure of his will leave her vulnerable. The text shows Lisa continually making moves towards Thatch and then conceals that movement. When she finds Thatch in the kitchen, she suddenly freezes; her movement is covered by his embrace. The text is quite clear that Lisa desires Thatch; what, therefore, is it avoiding here? Perhaps postponing is a better word. It postpones defining the nature of that desire: whether it is romantic or sexual. Yet what would it mean for the text to own up to the heroine's sexuality at such a stage in the proceedings? Wouldn't it position her as a hussy after only one thing, perhaps, or as being under passion's sway, out of control? Neither would be to the girl's advantage in the face of male power, and it is with that male power that the heroine must negotiate.

So the text comes face to face with its second centre of interest: the signification of male behaviour. If the boy is powerful, he is also suspect. If he is in a position to harm the girl, take advantage of her feelings, she must ensure her own safety. To do this she must scrutinise his intentions. To be safe, he must be moved by deep feelings which are more than sexual. For male sexuality can be read as simultaneously out of control – 'I couldn't help myself' – and detached, having no part in the man's emotional life. If Lisa is to give in to her own feelings, let her actions speak openly of them, Thatch must be moved in the same way, made equally vulnerable.

This seems to me to be the key to the whole issue. The text never hesitates over Lisa's feelings for Thatch, even as it refuses to define exactly what they might be. Instead, it concentrates on how those feelings might be read by others and what the implications of those readings might be for the achievement of the heroine's desire. The text alternates between revealing the girl's feelings for the boy (feelings which are established before her encounter with him), the boy's potential reading of those feelings (placed by sexuality or romance, contexts which themselves conflict) and the girl's view of his actions, as she weighs up his behaviour. The different ways in which the boy could interpret the girl's behaviour also become a means for the girl to scrutinise the boy. John Berger, in *Ways of Seeing*, drew attention to the way in which women incorporate the male view of themselves: 'Men look at women. Women watch themselves being looked at.' But in watching themselves being looked at, women also watch the watcher back.

The romance may operate as a way of evading questions about female sexuality, but it does so by opening up questions about the male power to name. The writer's attention is focused by the genre – not on sexuality as an ahistorical possibility outside culture, but, on the contrary, on boys' reading of that sexuality and on the space for female sexual desire in a world named by men. The male view of women, the female view of men, are seen as being in conflict. The woman's view of the man includes the knowledge that the man's view of her is wrong, and that if she succumbs without a struggle to his initial view of her, fails powerfully to contest it, she will be the loser. The heroine's job is to make the hero agree with her own estimation of herself. To write this sort of text the girl author must know what the boy's potential reading of her is. In bringing the text to its conclusion she must undercut his view by making him submit to the power of his own feelings.

Like Stephen's text, Joanna's deals with uncertainties, traces the possibilities of multiple readings, and circles around questions of power. Both writers' texts point outwards to a world of significatory practices in which the writers live. I am suggesting that their choice of genre is not accidental, that the reason why so many teenagers return to these forms again and again in their reading and writing is precisely because they bring into focus serious concerns. They are powerful because they can be set to work mapping out the complexities of the contexts within which young people act. They do so by depicting the tensions between alternative ways of reading masculinity (the thriller) or masculinity and femininity (the romance). The writers are neither wholly inside nor wholly outside the texts. Neither of them is recounting events which actually happened. They are exploring possible rules for an encounter, not in terms of action (skinheads getting crushed by a lorry or the other girl being ruthlessly humiliated) but in terms of meaning.

I want to return to the use I made earlier of Vygotsky, who saw action in play as subordinated to the meaning of things. I am arguing that in deploying the rules of writing, children struggle over the appropriation of discursive practices. These discursive practices would position them but do not offer a unitary self, one single position from which events can be securely interpreted. Rather, they are full of contradictions and conflicts. By deploying a particular genre and watching what it throws into relief young writers are speculating about the future and working out how it could be understood in terms of what they already know. They are playing with meaning.

What are the implications of these arguments for classroom practice? Most fundamentally, they suggest a need to change how we think about personal writing. I have outlined in the second chapter how teachers may imagine that personal writing is unmediated, a direct statement of the self which grows naturally out of experience. Given this view, teachers have tended to isolate as subjects for written work moments which they consider will have had particular importance in pupils' lives. The assumption here is that a powerful experience will in itself generate good writing. A look at examination titles or course books such as *Ourselves*, which are primarily concerned with personal writing, confirms this. The key moments selected are often associated with particularly strong feelings. Being frightened, having a bad dream, getting into trouble, a crisis in the family, being humiliated, losing, death, even boredom, are all seen as triggers for writing. Similarly, when it comes to choosing topics for discursive writing, subjects on which it is assumed young people will have strong views are also assumed to be easier to write about. So nuclear war, drugs and drug abuse and vandalism are all common topics. But having strong views or strong feelings does not in itself lead to 'good' writing. Just because a child is concerned about vandalism does not mean they can write a well-polished essay on the subject. Feeling very strongly about the death of a relative or losing an argument will not of itself lead to the coherent expression of those feelings in short-story form, complete with evocation of atmosphere and attention to detail. These are formal conventions shaped by a particular cultural history, not the neutral expression of the way things are.

Children cannot avoid using conventions when they write, but, as we've seen, the conventions they often deploy in their story-writing are those of popular fiction. Set the title 'Jealousy' for an examination essay, and the chances are that those answering the question will not write in intimate detail about, say, their feelings on the birth of a younger sister, but instead will use the romance genre to describe a fight over a boy or the adventure genre to describe rivalry between two street gangs. Part of the explanation for this sort of choice may simply be that children fail to recognise what else we have in mind. Why should they? We are rarely explicit about exactly what we do want, precisely because we assume that a powerful experience will in effect write itself, and needs no crafting.

At one level my argument is that if we want children to write in a particular manner we should at least let them know what the rules of such production are. When it comes to personal writing this is not as straightforward as it might seem. For instance, what are the rules for the production of a personal journal, a form increasingly finding favour with teachers and used in a variety of contexts? Learning to write a good personal journal is not a matter of being a particularly sensitive individual, but of mastering the way a particular form is structured. Similarly, learning to write well about literary texts must depend on more than teachers reading children texts which may be found personally moving, and then hoping that their students will feel the same way and that that shared feeling will of itself generate the sort of writing teachers want. What is the set of conventions which governs the production (and our recognition) of a sensitive personal response? Teachers need to be able to answer these sorts of questions if they are to help children to write.

I have been talking so far about how we can enable children to fulfil the criteria teachers may already have in mind when they come to set a writing task, but at another level we need to ask ourselves why we want children to write in this particular way. Why are teachers so preoccupied by personal writing? I have already drawn attention to the way in which teachers assume that the genres of popular fiction embody particular (homogeneous) values. If teachers don't like the set of values which is assumed to underlie the models of popular fiction that a writer has deployed they may well attempt to redirect their attention by getting them to think more closely about their own experience and then work from that. So, in relation to Stephen's piece, for instance, one might worry over the nature of the violence that is included and particularly over the amorality of the ending: the skinheads get crushed to death and the hero nonchalantly turns his bike and heads for home. It would be perfectly possible to imagine asking Stephen to rewrite this sort of piece by getting him to think back to a time in his own life when he had been chased or in danger. The assumption here would be that in describing 'real' events in detail, he would come up with something less melodramatic and in this way 'improve' the piece by re-creating it in other terms where the fact that violence is disturbing and unpleasant, and has frightening conse-quences, could be 'naturally' acknowledged.

My argument has been that the reality we seek to disclose in this way is just as much a matter of convention as the genres we seek to discard; it is no more natural, no more the product of the direct apprehension of experience than the texts we dislike. The alternative readings promoted in Media Studies, through anti-sexism and anti-racism and in the Leavisite approach to English are just as much a product of social, cultural and historical relations. I do not mean by this that we cannot therefore prefer one version to another, give priority to one account over the others. I am saying, though, that we cannot do so by appealing to nature, to what the child *really* knows. Indeed, looking at Joanna's and Stephen's texts shows just how futile an enterprise this would be, for in their writing, the real – what they know from first-hand experience – and the conventional – what they know from texts they have read – are inextricably mixed together, continually sliding over one another, subtly shifting the focus. And it is precisely the ways in which these alternative kinds of reading interact with each other to illuminate the matter in hand that have interested me.

In seeking to clear away the damagingly conventional (whether it is seen as warping the fineness of the human spirit, or promoting false consciousness) and to release the true potential of the child (their real experience) through encouraging personal writing, teachers assume that they are invoking a better set of values. Because we are so certain that particular forms carry with them particular sets of values, we use arguments about the form as a substitute for arguing about what we believe in.

Just as I do not think that Stephen is expressing a commitment to acts of violence in his own life by writing 'It was time to leave', so I do not believe that asking him to employ a different set of rules will involve him in appropriating wholesale another set of values. Writing fiction is not about the rehearsal of fixed moral positions. It does not reveal a single and uncomplicated truth about who the writer is, nor translate straightforwardly into action in the future. In suggesting that teachers make too many claims for the virtues of personal writing I am not arguing that we should dispense with it altogether. Instead, I would argue that we should broaden our notions of what constitutes useful and interesting writing, and include within that definition writing based on popular fiction. Once we start to take writing based on popular fiction seriously, there would be other consequences for our practice. We could encourage children to articulate what they already know about how such fictions work and help to refine that knowledge. At the same time, at least some of the difficulties children encounter in writing genre fiction are undoubtably due to the fact that the form they are striving to imitate often does not fit easily with the form their teachers give them to write in. It is difficult to reproduce a thriller or a science-fiction epic in the space of a short story. This mismatch currently only serves to compound the misunderstandings that already exist between teachers and pupils over what the formal requirements for any one piece of work are. Once we take popular fiction seriously as a model for children's writing, we might want to review the kind of writing tasks we set them as well as the variety of model texts we encourage them to read.

So far I have been arguing that we untie the connections we have made between form and value, but by paying attention to form I am not suggesting that we treat our pupils as if they were soulless technicians mastering an empty set of conventions. We do not need to return to the sort of practice that was common in the first half of this century, when the acquisition of a good style was seen to depend on children being able to work their way through the following sorts of exercises:

> **Endings of Sentences.** A sentence ought to end with strength, definition, and euphony. Consider the following:
>
>   (1) He spoke of him as a grand old English gentleman, possessing the attributes of generosity and modesty, rare nowadays.   *Daily Paper*
> This sentence ends badly, trailing off into the indefinite, and having a weak, halting sound when read aloud. Try the effect of –
>
>   He spoke of him as a grand old English gentleman, possessing the attributes, rare enough nowadays, of generosity and modesty.
>
>   . . .
>
>   (5) The month of May continues to behave like a spoilt child, bad-tempered storms being followed by alternate sunshine and tears.
>   *Daily Paper*
> A good ending, strong, definite, and euphonious. Would 'tears and sunshine' make a better ending, or is 'sunshine and tears' more suitable to the dominant thought of the sentence? (Wilson, Richard, 1925, pp. 28–9)

Devoid of any context except the invocation of an abstract standard of good style, this seems to be positively unhelpful where it is not incomprehensible. My interest in identifying the conventions of writing is not for their own sake, but for the ways in which they can be used to establish meaning. So in teaching the conventions we also need to be able to look more closely at the effects that are achieved as they are deployed within the context of any one piece. This might involve using some of the critical strategies commonly associated with Media Studies, asking such questions as: How does this piece come to have a meaning? What is its purpose, and how has it been produced? But we would do this for different reasons. Rather than using such questions to focus pupils' attention on how they are being manipulated or worked on by the text – constructing the text as all-powerful and themselves as powerless – the point would be to enable pupils to manipulate the rules of the text's construction for themselves. In other words, it would involve children in trying out what they have learnt from their reading in their own writing, for their own purposes. In one sense the teaching of writing must always be just this. We cannot escape from dealing with the rules of writing's production, for if they are to write at all, children must appropriate that knowledge.

Conversely, if the conventions of writing are inextricably linked with meaning, each is dependent on the other. In encouraging children to speak for themselves it is not enough to appeal to the 'spark of inventiveness', or their creative intentions shaped outside language. Invention is tied to the forms which we inherit, shaped by the social processes of culture and history. Thus, creative originality is not the solitary unique act of an inspired individual. What we recognise as creativity is writers acting back on the inherited form and in the process writing themselves into culture.

Meaning and form are inextricably interlinked. At the same time, in my analysis of Stephen's, Joanna's and Angelique's work, I have sketched out a much more tentative relationship between form and meaning than adult readers of children's writing normally allow for. Teachers too often imagine that in reproducing popular fictions children reproduce one solitary closed meaning. The genres of popular fiction are seen as bearing a single message, which effectively excludes any other questions we might want to ask. So the romance, for example, is denigrated because it is seen as teaching girls how to be overwhelmed by boys. In reproducing the romance girls are assumed to be accepting one particular position in relation to patriarchy: one of passive subordination. The confidence with which this view is expressed depends on our reading of the story's ending. We take that moment – Lisa's decision to accept Thatch, the narrator's escape from the skinheads – and work backwards from it to establish what the story is all about. In focusing on the completed product we have overlooked the process which produces it – a process which, I have suggested, is much more uncertain and incomplete than we have allowed for.

This assumption that some texts are committed to reproducing a single position is strongly argued by anti-sexists in their discussion of reading. The argument is most often rehearsed, though, in relation to particular sorts of texts: reading schemes and the genres of popular fiction, not good literature, which is an interesting point in itself. The argument hinges on the notion that politically unacceptable positions found in texts are quite easy to identify once you've adopted an anti-sexist framework. They are also regarded as particularly powerful and compelling. They have to be challenged or in some way interrupted if they are not to be swallowed wholesale by their readers. This leads to certain sorts of practice in relation to writing, most notably an attempt both to monitor and control the sorts of meaning children produce. My own initial comments on Joanna's story 'At the Party' reflect this. When I marked it for homework I wrote:

> Some punctuation errors, but this piece worked well. It was well organised and events led towards the climax. (Why is it always the girls fighting over the boys and not the other way round?)

My point is that in assuming the right to pass political judgements it is easy to make mistakes. Looking back at Joanna's story now I would say that my final comment was at best an irrelevance, at worst an implied criticism which the piece did not merit. I was concerned that in including the incident where Mel is roundly told to get lost, Joanna was implying that there was no virtue in female friendship and no possibility of female solidarity in the presence of boys. My rereading of the piece has led me to revise that judgement. 'At the Party' does not have female friendship as a central focus of interest and consequently has nothing to say about it as such. The incident with Mel functions instead as a way of drawing attention to the insecure nature of the encounter between girls and boys.

I am arguing that we cannot make up our minds about what a piece of writing means simply because we recognise a particular genre or a particular convention: girls fighting over a boy. Instead, meaning is produced by the way in which particular elements are recombined in each case. We have to think more carefully about where our own judgements come from before we jump to conclusions. What are the sets of value that we bring to the text? How do they influence our reading? As I've already pointed out, the ease with which it's possible to dismiss the romance has as much to do with the contempt of a sexist society for all things feminine as it has with the winning of an anti-sexist argument. Part of the problem I identified in my readings of Joanna's and Stephen's texts was precisely to do with how my own preconceptions made it difficult to avoid prejudging the issues. Negotiating my way through Joanna's and Stephen's texts meant negotiating also with myself and my own position in a patriarchal society. It meant recognising the different valuations I brought to my readings. What I am getting at here is that teachers are not immune in some way from the processes of culture. We are just as much involved and implicated as our pupils in working through the diverse ways of reading available to us.

I have been arguing that we should spend more time teaching about the conventions of writing and less time worrying about the conclusions we think children reach in their work. They are not rehearsing fixed positions, and there is every reason to believe that our estimations of the significance of their work are often wide of the mark. But does this mean that we effectively adopt a *laissez-faire* attitude in the classroom? That given the chance that we might make the wrong judgements, we just keep quiet and let each individual go their own way in the hope that everything will turn out all right in the end? In which case, whatever happens to questions of value and our concern for the pupils in our class? It sounds as if it could be a recipe for the worst sort of liberalism where, unable to take a strong line on anything, teachers abnegate all responsibility for the way things turn out. If this happened, wouldn't it follow that, left to their own devices, those children most vulnerable to the dominant meanings within our society would simply go under? But who is most at risk here? The anti-sexist and anti-racist positions suggest that it is girls and Blacks. However, my argument about writing rests on the notion that the sets of cultural knowledge that children use in their writing are not homogeneous but diverse and full of contradictions. The meanings that can be established are multiple not unitary and are temporarily achieved, not permanently fixed. This has important consequences for my understanding of what happens in the encounter between the powerful and the powerless, both within and outside our classrooms.

To explain what I mean, let me briefly reflect on the Post-Structuralist argument on which I have drawn in much of this book. For the Post-Structuralists, experience is always mediated by language, which is in itself unstable. However, there are some problems with the way the Post-Structuralist view gets taken up outside the confines of the philosophical debate where it originally emerged. In arguing their case for the primacy of language, much of the Post-Structuralists' time is taken up with exposing just what a slippery fish language is. For the Post-Structuralist, the meaning which any one text achieves is an effect of the language which is deployed, and that meaning is always on the point of collapse, defined as much by what it excludes, keeps out of sight, as by what it reveals. At the same time as it draws attention to language, therefore, this approach also treats it with suspicion. Deconstruction – the name given to the methods Post-Structuralists use to take texts apart – has proved useful to those already committed to conspiracy theories, for it suggests that everything that is said should be distrusted, the only truth that counts being the one that remains unspoken. At the same time, it has proved equally useful to those committed to a relativist outlook. If all texts are equally untrue (in an absolute sense), then it doesn't matter what anyone says; everything has equal merit.

My own interest in Post-Structuralism is different. Let me take as a starting point the idea of discourse as defined by Catherine Belsey:

> A *discourse* is a domain of language-use, a particular way of talking (and writing and thinking). A discourse involves certain shared assumptions which appear in the formulations that characterize it. The discourse of common sense is quite distinct, for instance, from the discourse of modern physics, and some of the formulations of the one may be expected to conflict with the formulations of the other. (Belsey, Catherine, 1980, p. 5)

If any one body of statements (discourses) excludes as much as it includes, then I would say that it *partially* illuminates – it is neither the complete truth, nor complete lies. It is a temporary resting point, which throws some things into relief even as it disguises others. There is, therefore, no point in looking for a complete and all-inclusive statement about the way the world is. We can only ever make do with the provisional statements we have to hand. At the same time, the spaces between different discourses, their partiality, their very incompleteness, guarantees that they will change. What we argue for today, we will jettison later.

What does all this have to do with the relationship between the powerful and the powerless? My point is that when it comes to manoeuvring between different discourses it is the powerless, those most commonly excluded from the dominant discourses, who seem to me to have the advantage. For rather than seeking to maintain the ways things look now, they have most to gain from exploiting the contradictions, the gaps and the silences which result from language's inability to fix meaning once and for all. The position I am putting forward here takes me quite close to the argument Liz Stanley and Sue Wise make in their book *Georgie Porgie*. In talking about sexual harassment they point out that it is not good enough to divide up men into those who do harass, abuse or belittle women and those who don't, as if one could somehow sort out the right-on men from the rest. Their point is that all men have the potential to do power or to do sexism over women by virtue of the cultural materials that are to hand. They use the expressions 'doing power' and 'doing sexism', because this makes clear that these are processes rather than fixed attributes. They are effects which have to be achieved rather than automatically assumed:

> 'Sexism' is actually very complex: what women know very well is that a man opening a door for us can be sexist patronage or kindness or indeed *both*, for social behaviour is multi-dimensional. (Wise, Sue and Stanley, Liz, 1987, p. 151)

If power is the outcome of a particular encounter, men's power is therefore always open to dispute:

> Conventional interpretations of 'women's oppression' see it as a state in which women are totally powerless and men have all the power that exists ... We don't accept [this] view of reality, and of men, women and power, that this closed system describes. We see women's oppression as an end result, a final product of a complex process in which men attempt to do power, and sometimes succeed and sometimes don't, and women resist and undermine and are often successful. (Ibid., pp. 160–61)

They go on to outline some of the different strategies women use in fighting back against sexual harassment, grouping them under headings: reacting against; joining in; letting it pass and avoiding it. They make the point that only the first strategy is generally recognised as women challenging men, but add that the others may be just as effective in particular circumstances. Moreover, they suggest that it is not possible to define what a successful strategy should be outside the context of a particular encounter.

All this seems to have taken me rather far away from classrooms and questions of what teachers should do about children's writing. But there are connections – most importantly, that it makes more sense for teachers to spend less time prescribing how girls should behave by devising anti-sexist strategies and more time supporting girls in what they are already up to. In other words, we should be adopting a pro-woman line. A feminist strategy could be anything that negates men's or boys' 'doing power' over women. If we want to harass anybody about what they write, what they say and what they do in the way much anti-sexist teaching suggests we might as well stick to the boys. Who knows? Maybe they would recognise that sort of behaviour as precisely the sort of 'doing power' that they attempt to apply to others?

I am suggesting that the diversity of discourses works to the advantage of those who are marginalised by the dominant discourses and to the disadvantage of those who would maintain a position of power, itself a temporary and uncertain achievement. By drawing attention to the contradictions between the different sets of knowledge that children use in their writing we can open up questions about power and questions about difference: about masculinity and feminity. In other words, if we are serious about our politics it is not so much a matter of coming to the classroom with a fixed position, a set of ready-made answers, as setting the agenda for the discussion and facilitating, through our support of the girls, how that discussion will take place.

To illustrate what I mean I want briefly to describe a particular lesson I had with the fourth-year group of which Angelique, Joanna and Stephen were members. I had previously asked the class to write for homework as realistic an account of the sort of talk that went on in small groups during registration as they could manage, with this proviso: they were to restrict themselves to the sort of talk that went on in single-sex groups and were to begin with their own sex. Once they had done this they were to go on and write down what they imagined the conversation would be like between members of the opposite sex in the same circumstances. So each individual wrote two pieces, one entitled 'Girls' Talk', one entitled 'Boys' Talk': one piece drawing on what they knew from first hand, the other speculative. In this particular lesson, the tasks having been completed, I divided the blackboard into four columns. Two were headed girls' talk, two were headed boys' talk, and we began to write down all the subjects that had been mentioned by the class in their writing. In this way we began to collect an impression both of what the girls and the boys had actually been talking about and what they thought the other sex would have been talking about. What emerged was as follows: the girls thought the boys would have been talking about sex and violence. The boys described themselves as talking about sex and violence, although they had also talked about hobbies (something the girls hadn't thought of).

> 'Geoff', Neil and I shouted in unison as Geoff walked through the door.
> 'Ah', as Geoff heaved his bag off his back, '... caught three chubb yesterday, down Keynsham.'
> 'Oh yea', said Neil.
> 'Yea', said Geoff, 'I've frozen them. You can see 'em tonight if you want.'
> 'You're on. Coming tonight Rich?'
> 'Might as well. Nothing else to do.'
> 'Call about 5', said Geoff. 'After I'll get my radio-controlled car out'

The boys thought the girls would have been talking about boyfriends, pop groups and records.

> 'Hello Sarah', said Catherine as she walked in
> 'Right. Hey I got my Wham fan club letter back today', said Debby
> 'Hey, what did it say?'
> 'Well it said all about their coming tour and ...'
> 'Hey guess what', said Louise running in, 'Jeremy is going out with that new girl. You know, the one with spots all over her neck and the fat legs'
> 'How could he stand it' said Sarah
> 'How could she stand it' said Debby
> 'How could they stand it' said Louise

None of the girls had described themselves as talking about pop groups. They had described themselves as talking about boyfriends, but they had also covered a much wider array of topics: clothes, friends, teachers, homework, parents, watching television, buying presents. The list went on. But at the same time there was a common thread running through much of what they wrote about. Almost regardless of the subject matter, the conversation would be used to define relationships.

> 'Me and Christine went up Kingswood on Saturday, right?' Sharon said to me. 'I bought a chip-fryer for my Mum and a big doll for my sister and I made Christine carry it all the way home'

'Yeh, they were really heavy and I couldn't see where I was going and I hit my head,' said Christine. 'And Sharon just stood there laughing.'

Alison then came into the room and told a dirty joke.

'My Mum nearly hit me when I told her it' she said after.

'I should think she did' Christine replied.

It was once we'd established these broader headings that the conversation became interesting. At first the boys were quite happy to have the subjects of their discussion listed as sex, violence and hobbies. The mention of sex and violence produced loud laughter and a variety of other noises from the boys in the class. But as the conversation developed around the differences between the boys' treatment of these subjects and the complexity of the girls' writing, other things began to happen. The girls became increasingly restless, both impatient with the way the boys had underestimated what they were up to and critical of the topics the boys had chosen. This culminated in Angelique turning round to the boys and saying: 'The trouble with you lot is you just haven't got any feelings.' In the rather stunned silence that followed I picked on the one boy in the class who I thought would be prepared to give me a straight answer and said: 'That's a very serious charge. What have you got to say about it?' Suddenly the whole tenor of the conversation changed. The boy began to talk about how difficult it was to express your feelings as a boy talking to other boys, how the pressure was on to disguise the feelings you have, or if you couldn't do that, show them through violence. The whole basis for the boys' pride in their ability to talk about sex and violence had been undercut.

That is the brief outline of the lesson. Now let me consider in more detail just what was going on here. When the boys wrote about what they imagined the girls' talk to be, they wrote about it with contempt. Richard, whose piece of girls' talk I quoted from above, had this comment to make when, following the lesson, I asked the class to summarise the discussion that had gone on under the heading 'The differences between boys' and girls' talk':

> Girls talk about boyfriends and how well they get on with them. Also they talk about more trivial things than boys and things which are less important. Girls always seem to talk about clothes right down to the last detail. Boys like being fashionable but girls are more fussy.

The underlying assumptions behind the sorts of topics that the boys chose for the girls were that these considerations were trivial and not serious. At the same time they also misrepresented how the girls actually talked about boyfriends. They imagined that such talk was either about status (so Jeremy can be mocked for going out with an unglamorous girl) or revealed the girls as being fixated on the boys (given over to their power?) or showed them to be soppy (given over to feelings) unlike the 'hard' boys. Here is Richard again:

> The main difference in boys' and girls' talk is that boys think about the rougher side of life and girls think about appearance and relationships more.

So in other words, in their account of girls' talk the boys were attempting to 'do power' over the girls. When it came to discussing what they had written in the lesson, the boys' initial concern was both to show that they were different from the girls and to show that the girls' concerns weren't up to much, but in the process of the discussion the girls became increasingly vociferous in refusing the boys' valuation of them. They were trying to get out of the position in which the boys were trying to place them and to defend their own interests against the boys. I went along with what was going on and supported the girls by encouraging them to look at what they themselves had written, and to find ways of validating it. I did this both by asking them to reflect direcly on their own work – 'How is what you've written about different?' – and by giving them the space in the discussion to do so – in other words, shutting up the boys.

The key to the radical shift in the conversation came when Angelique directly challenged the boys about what they were up to by applying the criteria the girls had established in their own work to the boys. By saying that this was a very serious charge and insisting that a particular individual answered it rather than dismissing it, I changed the whole grounds of the discussion. Now the boys had to reconsider what they had been talking about from another perspective, one which had been identified as the girls'. The outcome was that the girls got their own power back and refused the boys' definition of them, whilst the boys had the opportunity to rethink their own position in different terms.

What was the gap in the discourse which allowed this to happen? In the version of their own talk that they had given in their writing the boys had been pushing away feelings so that they could rehearse a strong objective masculinity, dealing in the impersonal. In so doing they were claiming adult male status. Their version of boys talking about girls was to talk about girls as sex objects, rather than who they were interested in going out with and how they might manage that: 'Angela's a bit of all right. Cor, what a pair of knockers.' In writing about violence they were most interested in establishing the status of the participants according to who was most prepared to throw punches:

> 'Did you see that scrap last week? Terry really gave it to him. You should have seen the blood. Paul got it right on the nose.'

But in saying this they were not giving the complete truth about themselves. They were covering over certain areas of their lives in an attempt to give a strong public performance which could establish their status in relation to the other boys. At times their writing showed another side to the way things were, even if only by implication. Richard's piece of conversation, which had been summed up under the heading 'Hobbies', is also in an oblique way about friendship. Even if the tone is casual – 'Coming tonight Rich?' 'Might as well. Nothing else to do,' – it's also about being friends and the relationships between boys. In a way the boys' biggest mistake, which was ultimately to lead to them failing to 'do power' over the girls, was in accepting the summary of their agenda as sex, violence and hobbies. They accepted it because it looked impersonal and also made them look big. In their own terms handling these subjects in rather racy conversation was proof of the masculinity to which they aspired. It was what made them different from the girls:

> If someone notices boys have feelings and consideration for girls they will call them soppy and other stuff. So just to prove to their mates, when the girl isn't around he will talk about her with his mates saying 'Oh, she's all right, but a bit of a cow at times'. ... Boys don't involve girls in their conversations because they think she wouldn't know what she was talking about. If it was a girls' conversation he wouldn't be interested because if he was his mates would call him sissy.

> Boys think about the rougher side of life and girls think about appearance and relationships more. The rougher side of life is horror films, rough sports and fighting, etc. Also things like cars and bikes, etc., are often talked about.

But it was also their undoing because this impersonal agenda is not a complete representation of who the boys are, and once questions had been raised by the girls about feelings, the boys' bluff had been called. So the terms of the conversation were switched by drawing attention back to what the boys were trying to exclude. Instead of trying to argue with what was there in the boys' talk – this sex and violence is repulsive – the girls won back the agenda by pointing to what was absent in the boys' talk: feelings. They identified the absence by establishing the difference between what was present in their own work and what was present in the boys', but also by taking their own work as the norm against which the boys' could be judged. It was this sort of positive comparison between the two that pushed the discourse over into something new.

Of course that doesn't mean to say that the particular strategy the girls used here will always work, nor that it is the only one, but it does indicate that a useful starting point can be found by exploiting the differences between perspectives in our pupils' writing. Too often as teachers we have been misled by the text's closure into overlooking the process which preceded it: the text's silences, its gaps, its hesitations, its falterings; the writers' activity as they duck and weave, balance and pivot between conflicting readings. In so doing we have missed out on the chance to open up for discussion those very points which we claimed to be seeking, and perhaps most importantly on the chance to start talking about those issues in the places where they matter most, where the children themselves have sited them. If texts reflect the partial agenda of discursive practices lived out in real life, contradictory and uncertain, both powerfully and yet fragilely constituted, then there is much to be gained by teachers exploiting that diversity. Rather than offering our pupils a fixed and unaltering position, we should be facilitating the exchange of meanings, and dealing with difference.

Appendix

OH STEVE!!!

'Don't tell me what to do son!' I shouted at Steve 'You 'ave got a bloody nerve, telling me what to do' I walked off down the lane. That took a lot of courage telling Steve that. You see Steve my ... well boyfriend had been seeing me, and about 10 other girls, boys as well I bet! I wouldn't be surprised. Everybody else saw him more than I did and I was going out with him!

Steve was what I would call 'lush' but there are of course more suitable and maybe not so common names to call him. It was Lisa and Claire that introduced him to me, when I was young, tender, and realise now, bloody stupid! I couldn't see anyone else but Steve, I couldn't communicate with anyone else except Steve. I was going out with Steve for a steady 14 months.

Anyway today Steve really got what they called the goat. Before I was quite prepared to share him with whoever wanted him too, even though I was meant to be seeing him. I really loved him. I just really loved him. Most of my mates said I was stupid.

It all really started when I had been invited ... oh and Steve (of course) to an Engagement Party, Lisa and Mark's, of course I was shocked and surprised at Lisa for inviting me and Steve, because Steve and Lisa hate each other because of the way he used me, she hated seeing me get hurt.

'I'm only inviting him because of you' she said, but then she would do that for me, a good friend, Lisa. She invited us about 2 weeks before it had even got around.

Anyway I shan't go on anymore here we are (me and Steve) 2 weeks before the party.

I had gone down to Steve's to call for him, bloody ridiculous I know, he could at least come down for me but then I've always been treated like a mug. Well it was of course pouring down with rain. It unusually always has been raining since I've been going out with Steve. I rapped on the door, the rain beating down on my umbrella. I felt really comfortable and wet, a bit like a tap. His mother opened the door.

'Hello Ange love, he's in bed still.'

'Oh?' I said raving mad with anger inside.

'Go up and wake him, lazy sod' She let me in.

'Ever since he's been on the dole, he's been in bed. While I've been working you've been at school, he's been in bed!' Well she kept on and on but I didn't pay much attention. I was mad at the fact that I was on holiday and he was in bed, he ought to be bringing glad tidings to me, me in my bed! (If you get what I mean!!!)

I walked in his room and shut the door (well maybe I slammed it) and he turned over with his eyes closed and mumbled.

'Oh muh, let I get some kip I'm knackered' Well sorry lads but anger was just welling up inside me, him lying there loving that morning rest and me, yes me, soaked to death from a lovely shower God had sent me (he must of thought I needed it). I looked around his room not a pleasant sight I can assure you. A page 3 girl hanging over his bed and his clothes on the floor, money in great quantities on his chair beside the bed. I was mad really mad. I walked over to the dressing table and picked up some aftershave that he had never used (which I don't blame him it stank) I opened the bottle, with some doubts I must admit, and poured it all over his sleeping face.

'Ugh, pooh, poof, bloody ... **!**! what the bloody hell do you think your doing.'

'I'm bloody sick of being mugged by you, treating me like your bleedin' pet dog! How do you think I feel? having to share you with about 50 other slags not that I'm one, but I'm being treated as though I am. Well Steve Ridgely you can bloody forget it. It's over you and me, over. You're a real bastard and I hate you. There's millions of other guys who want to go with me and now I want to go with them.'

During this great speech, he didn't get a chance to speak, he was wiping his face, and the bedroom stank of 'Karate' the aftershave that turns women wild! they were bloody right 'n' all!!! I turned and headed for the door, 'Ange wait' Steve called me.

'What?' I said looking at him. His mum had just slammed the door, she was on her way to work, we were alone in the house. 'Oh Ange don't be mad. I worked all day yesterday' he said with his usual morning mumble.

'Oh yeah. What, took you all day to read the sports page? Oh yeah gawping at page 3 was probably overtime' I was really angry.

'No truthfully, I've started a YOP Scheme now, down this centre' he told me.

'How come your mum didn't tell me?' I asked him.

''Cause she don't know either, I'm saving some money' He said. I stared at him wondering whether he was lying or not.

'What about this morning' I said to him.

'Don't do it today, only Weds, Fris.'

'Lyin' sod' I shouted.

'No truthfully, Ange' I looked at his piteful face and wanted to crumble it like a paper bag.

'Well at least get up then' I said to him.

'I can't.' He said smirking.

'Why' I said putting my hands on my hips.

'This is why.' He got up ... my mind went blank for a second through shock. He was absolutely starkers, nude, naked, bare completely!

I tried not to look embarassed as he climbed back in bed.

'What ... what was that trying to prove?' I felt as if I was sinking in the ground.

'Nothing.' He smirked 'I've been seeing you for 14 months you might as well see me,' he lit a fag.

'Why? Your not getting your eyeful off me' I said.

'Don't you trust me to be careful?'

I knew he had changed the subject too quickly. Everything was said too quickly. And we all should know what happened after persuading a little.

'You deserve an eternity ring for that.' he produced a ring. Oh a lovely ring, the most expensive thing he's ever bought me.

I was so happy I never regretted a thing I had done. I made Steve his breakfast and after he had washed the aftershave blended together making him smell really nice. I then kissed him, that made me realise how soppy I was towards him, love wise, I mean I thought love was all mills and boons book reader for Mark and Lisa, Claire and Karl not for me and Steve.

Things got really better for a couple of weeks especially in school, I walked around waving my flash eternity ring and listened to Lisa calling me a 'love sick fool'. I knew Lisa would of said that, that's why I had a funny feeling in my stomach and I knew it wasn't pregnancy.

I knew it, one day Steve and I would argue again, he started using me like his mug. All he seemed to want to talk about was Sex, sex all the time and one day he ordered me like his slave to let him have his own way with me. I'm not one for women's lib or burning the bra but him telling me what to do sex wise is going too far. So . . . it ended. Sadly I couldn't really argue with, but I know one thing, I miss him like hell!

Bibliography

Allen, David, *English Teaching Since 1965 How Much Growth?* (1980) Heinemann Educational Books.

Ang, Ien, *Watching Dallas: Soap Opera and the Melodramatic Imagination* (1985) Methuen.

Associated Examining Board, Reports of Examiners June Examination 1961, Section 2 (1961).

Associated Examining Board, Reports of Examiners June Examination 1980 Section 2 (1980).

Associated Examining Board, Reports of Examiners June Examination 1981 Section 2 (1981).

Baines, Bridget, 'Literature and Sex-Bias in the Secondary School English Curriculum', in *Alice in Genderland* (1985) NATE.

Bantock, G. H. *Studies in the History of Educational Theory*, vol. I. *Artifice and Nature 1350–1765* (1980) Allen & Unwin.

Barker, Martin, *A Haunt of Fears* (1984) Pluto Press.

Barthes, Roland, *Mythologies* (1973) Paladin.

Barthes, Roland, *S/Z* (1974) Hill & Wang.

Barthes, Roland, *Image-Music-Text* (1977) Fontana/Collins.

Batsleer, Janet *et al.*, *Rewriting English* (1985) Methuen.

Belsey, Catherine, *Critical Practice* (1980) Methuen.

Berger, John, *Ways of Seeing* (1972) Penguin.

Bethell, Andrew, 'Media Studies' in Miller, Jane (ed.), *Eccentric Propositions* (1984) Routledge & Kegan Paul.

Beveridge, M. (ed.), *Children Thinking through Language* (1982) Edward Arnold.

Bolgar, R. R. 'Humanist Education and its Contribution to the Renaissance', in History of Education Society (ed.), *The Changing Curriculum* (1971).

Britton, James, *Language and Learning* (1970) Penguin.

Brooker, Peter, 'Post-structuralism, reading and the crisis in English', in Widdowson, P. (ed.), *Re-Reading English* (1982) Methuen.

Brownstein, Rachel M., *Becoming a Heroine* (1984) Penguin.

Buckingham, David, 'Teaching about the media: a rationale', *Secondary Education Journal*, vol. 15, no. 2. June 1985.

Buckingham, David, 'Against demystification', *Screen*, vol. 27, no. 5. Sept.–Oct. 1986.

Buckingham, David, 'Teaching about the media', in David Lusted (ed.), *The Media Studies Book: A guide for teachers* (1989, forthcoming) Comedia.

Buckingham, David, 'What is Media Studies' Pedagogy?,' paper presented to British Film Institute Education Department Seminar (1987).

Bullock, A. and Stallybrass, O. (eds), *The Fontana Dictionary of Modern Thought* (1977) Fontana.

Cawelti, John, *Adventure, Mystery, and Romance: Formula Stories as Art and Popular Culture* (1976) University of Chicago.

Coward, Rosalind and Ellis, John, *Language and Materialism* (1977) Routledge & Kegan Paul.

Derrida, J., *Positions* (1981) University of Chicago.

Derrida, J., *Writing and Difference* (1979) Routledge & Kegan Paul.

DES, *A Language for Life* (1975) HMSO.

Dixon, Bob, *Catching Them Young 1: Sex, Race and Class in Children's Fiction* (1977) Pluto Press.

Dixon, John and Stratta, Leslie, 'Achievements in Writing at 16+' (1981) University of Birmingham.

Dunsbee, Tony and Ford, Terry, *Mark my Words: A study of teachers as correctors of children's writing* (1980) Ward Lock Educational with NATE.

Eagleton, Terry, *Literary Theory* (1983) Basil Blackwell.

Eisenstein, Hester, *Contemporary Feminist Thought* (1984) Unwin.

Foucault, Michel, *The Archaeology of Knowledge* (1972) Tavistock.

Foucault, Michel, *The History of Sexuality* (1978) New York Pantheon.

Frith, Gill, 'Little Women, Good Wives', in Hunt, P. *et al.* (eds), *The English Curriculum: Gender* The English Centre.

Gallop, Jane, *Feminism and Psychoanalysis: The Daughter's Seduction* (1982) Macmillan.

Gaskell, Carole, ' "Frills, tea sets, dolls": reflections on teaching in a girls' school', in Hunt, P. *et al.* (eds), *The English Curriculum: Gender*, The English Centre.

George, Susan, *How the Other Half Dies* (1976) Penguin.

Graves, Donald, *Writing: Teachers and Children at Work* (1983) Heinemann Educational Books.

Hall, Stuart *et al.* (eds), *Culture, Media, Language* (1980) Hutchinson and CCCS.

Harland, Linda, 'Why doesn't Johnny skip? Or a look at female roles in reading schemes', in *Alice in Genderland* (1985) NATE.

Harland, Richard, *Superstructuralism: The Philosophy of Structuralism and Post-Structuralism* (1987) Methuen.

Harris, John and Wilkinson, Jeff (eds), *Reading Children's Writing: A Linguistic View* (1986) Allen & Unwin.

Hawkes, Terence, *Structuralism and Semiotics* (1977) Methuen.

History of Education Society (ed.), *The Changing Curriculum* (1971) Methuen.

Hoggart, Paul, 'Comics and magazines for schoolchildren', in Miller, Jane (ed.), *Eccentric Propositions* (1984) Routledge & Kegan Paul.

Hunt, P. *et al.* (eds), *The English Curriculum: Gender*, The English Centre.

Iser, Wolfgang, *The Act of Reading* (1978) Routledge & Kegan Paul.

Jackson, David, *Encounters with Books: Teaching Fiction 11–16* (1983) Methuen.

Johnston, Brian, *Assessing English: Helping Students to Reflect on Their Work* (1987) Open University Press and St Clair Press.

Kemp, Gene, *The Turbulent Term of Tyke Tyler* (1979) Penguin.

Klein, Gillian, *Reading into Racism: Bias in Children's Literature and Learning Materials* (1985) Routledge & Kegan Paul.

Kress, Gunter, *Learning to Write* (1982) Routledge & Kegan Paul.

Leavis, F. R. and Thompson, D., *Culture and Environment* (1948) Chatto & Windus.

Lee, V. J. (ed.), *English Literature in Schools* (1986) Open University Press.

Leggett, Jane and Hemming, Judith, 'Teaching Magazines', *The English Magazine*, no. 12, Spring 1984, pp. 8–14.

McRobbie, Angela and McCabe, Trish (eds), *Feminism for Girls: An adventure story* (1981) Routledge & Kegan Paul.

McRobbie, Angela, 'Jackie: An Ideology of Adolescent Femininity', in Waites, B. *et al.* (eds), *Popular Culture: Past and Present* (1982) Croom Helm, London, and Open University Press.

McRobbie, Angela and Nava, Mica, *Gender and Generation* (1984) Macmillan.

Martin, Nancy *et al.*, *Writing and Learning Across the Curriculum 11–16* (1976) Ward Lock Educational.

Masterman, Len, *Teaching about Television* (1980) Macmillan.

May, Sue, 'Story in its writeful place', in Miller, Jane (ed.), *Eccentric Propositions* (1984) Routledge & Kegan Paul.

Miller, Jane (ed.), *Eccentric Propositions* (1984) Routledge & Kegan Paul.

Miller, Jane, *Women Writing About Men* (1986) Virago.

Miller, Jean Baker, *Toward A New Psychology of Women* (1987) Allen Lane.

Modleski, Tania, *Loving with a Vengeance* (1984) Methuen.

NATE, *Alice in Genderland: Reflections on Language, Power and Control* (1985).

Neale, Stephen, *Genre* (1980) British Film Institute.

Protherough, Robert, *Encouraging Writing* (1983) Methuen.

Radford, Jean (ed.), *The Progress of Romance* (1986), Routledge & Kegan Paul.

Radway, Janice A., 'Women Read the Romance: The interaction of Text and Context', *Feminist Studies*, vol. 9, no. 1. Spring 1983.

Radway, Janice A., *Reading the Romance* (1984) University of North Carolina Press.

Reeves, Frank and Chevannes, Mel, 'The Ideological Construction of Black Underachievement', *Multiracial Education*, no. 4 (1981/2).

Richmond, Chris, 'Classroom Readings', *Screen Education*, no. 4 (1981/2).

Richmond, John, 'What do 87 girls read?', *The English Magazine*, no. 1 (1979).

Richmond, John, 'What do 170 boys read?', *The English Magazine*, no. 5 (1980).

Richmond, John *et al.* (eds), *The English Curriculum: Writing*, The English Centre.

Root, Jane, *Pictures of Women* (1984) Pandora Press.

Rosen, Harold, *Stories and Meanings* (n.d.) NATE.

Russ, Joanna, *How to Suppress Women's Writing* (1983) The Women's Press.

Saussure, Ferdinand de, *Course in General Linguistics* (1974) Fontana.

Searle, John, 'Chomsky's Revolution in Linguistics', *The New York Review*, 29 June 1972.

Southern University Joint Board for School Examinations, Examinations for the General Certificate of Education Summer 1967 Examiners' Reports (1967).

Southern University Joint Board for School Examinations, Examinations for the General Certificate of Education Summer 1985 Examiners' Reports (1985).

Southern University Joint Board for School Examinations, Examinations for the General Certificate of Education Summer 1986 Examiners' Reports (1986).

Stanley, Liz and Wise, Sue, *Breaking Out: Feminist Consciousness and Feminist Research* (1983) Routledge & Kegan Paul.

Stanley, Liz, 'Whales and Minnows: Some Sexual Theorists and Their Followers and How They Contribute to Making Feminism Invisible', *Women's Studies International Forum*, vol. 7, no. 1 (1984), pp. 53–62.

Steedman, Carolyn, *The Tidy House* (1982) Virago.

Stephens, John, 'If it's a fragile it must be a girl', in Hunt, P. *et al.* (eds), *The English Curriculum: Gender*, The English Centre.

Stewig, J. W., *Exploring Language with Children* (1974) Colombus, Ohio.

Stones, Rosemary, *Pour out the Cocoa, Janet* (1983) Longmans.

Taylor, Hazel, 'Autobiography', in *The English Curriculum: Writing*, The English Centre.

Thornton, Geoffrey, *Teaching Writing: The Development of Written Language Skills* (1980) Edward Arnold.

University of London, Subject Reports June 1978 Examinations, (1978).

University of London, Subject Reports June 1984 Examinations, (1984).

Urwin, Cathy, 'The contribution of non-visual communication systems and language to knowing oneself', in Beveridge (ed.), *Children Thinking Through Language* (1982) Edward Arnold.

Volosinov, V. N., *Marxism and the Philosophy of Language* (1986) Harvard University Press.

Vygotsky, Lev Semenovitch, *Thought and Language* (1962) MIT Press.

Vygotsky, Lev Semenovitch, *Mind in Society* (1978) Harvard University Press.

Walkerdine, Valerie, 'Sex, power and pedagogy', *Screen Education*, no. 38. Spring 1981.

Walkerdine, Valerie, 'From context to text: a psychosemiotic approach to abstract thought', in Beveridge, M. (ed.) *Children Thinking Through Language* (1982) Edward Arnold.

Walkerdine, Valerie, 'Some Day my Prince Will Come: Young Girls and the Preparation for Adolescent Sexuality', in McRobbie, A. *et al.* (eds), *Gender and Generation* (1984).

West, Alastair, 'The Limits of a Discourse', *The English Magazine*, no. 18. Summer 1987.

White, Janet, *The Assessment of Writing: Pupils Aged 11 and 15* (1986) NFER-NELSON, Windsor.

Whitehead, Frank, *The Disappearing Dais: A study of the principles and practice of English teaching* (1966) Chatto & Windus Educational.

Wilkinson, Andrew (ed.), *The Writing of Writing* (1986) Open University Press.

Williamson, Judith, 'How Does Girl Number Twenty Understand Ideology', *Screen Education*, no. 40 (1981/2).

Willis, Paul, 'The Motor-Bike and Motor-Bike Culture' in Waites, B. *et al.* (eds), *Popular Culture: Past and Present* (1982) Croom Helm, London, and Open University Press.

Wilson, Richard, *English, Spoken and Written: A Graduated Course for Schools in Four Parts: Part IV* (1925) Thomas Nelson & Sons.

Wise, Sue and Stanley, Liz, *Georgie Porgie* (1987) Pandora Press.

Worpole, Ken, *Reading by Numbers: Contemporary Publishing and Popular Fiction* (1984) Comedia.

Worpole, Ken, *Dockers and Detectives* (1983).

Index

THE EDUCATION SERIES
In association with the University of London Institute of Education
Series Editor JANE MILLER

In recent years the attacks on education in Britain have meant a complete redrawing of the educational map. But attempts to stifle opposition and resistance have neither silenced nor deterred those who are doing innovatory work in every aspect of the field. In support of this radical tradition, Virago has launched a new education series, published in association with the University of London Institute of Education, committed to providing information and understanding of the social, cultural and developmental issues of significance in education today. It presents some of the most exciting and important thinking in ways which will appeal to professionals as well as to students and parents and all those for whom education is a central and continuing concern. The books are by teachers and researchers and originate from classrooms in schools and colleges, from the practices of teaching and the experiences of learning. The series' general editor is Jane Miller, Senior Lecturer in the Joint Department of English and Media Studies at the Institute of Education. The first three launch titles are: COUNTING GIRLS OUT by The Girls and Mathematics Unit, Institute of Education, compiled by Valerie Walkerdine; TEACHING BLACK LITERATURE by Suzanne Scafe and UN/POPULAR FICTIONS by Gemma Moss.

COUNTING GIRLS OUT
Girls and Mathematics Unit, Institute of Education

Compiled by Valerie Walkerdine

The question of girls' attainment in mathematics is met with
every kind of myth, false 'evidence', and theorising about the
gendered body and the gendered mind. The Girls and Mathematics Unit has, over a period of ten years, carried out detailed
theoretical and empirical investigations in this area. In taking
issue with truisms such as: women are irrational, illogical and
too close to their emotions to be any good at mathematics, this
study examines and puts into historical perspective claims made
about women's minds. It analyses the relationship between
evidence and explanation: why are girls still taken to be lacking
when they perform well, and boys taken to possess something
even when they perform poorly? *Counting Girls Out* is an enquiry
into the bases of these assumptions; it contains examples of work
carried out with girls, their teachers and their families – at home
and in the classroom – and discusses the problems and possibilities of feminist research more generally.

TEACHING BLACK LITERATURE

Suzanne Scafe

In examining the role of literature in a multicultural curriculum Suzanne Scafe challenges the literary tradition in education and the criteria by which texts enter that tradition. She argues for the urgent need to review the early initiatives within the education system which prompted the change from a monocultural approach to teaching to a multicultural approach, and discusses how these strategies for change are flawed: for example, it is not enough to introduce a few Black texts in what is little more than a tokenistic gesture. This becomes, for Black students, an experience of being patronised by the school, the curriculum and the teachers. Suzanne Scafe stresses how crucial the task is for educationalists to ensure that Black writing is valued critically: that it is read, both as a cultural and artistic whole and as a reflection of the political and cultural struggles which give it its context.

Announcing two new Education Series titles to be published in Spring 1990:

WASTING GIRLS' TIME
The Problem of Home Economics

Dena Attar

Wasting Girls' Time, a critical examination of the history and current status of domestic subjects in schools, looks at why and how these subjects were first included in school curricula, their subsequent effect on girls' education as a whole, and what feminist opposition to them has been. It also focuses on the struggles of domestic science pioneers and their modern counterparts to defend, upgrade and modernise their subject in spite of their low status, and the subject's identity as the domain of girls and women. It explores where boys fit in, what courses they are offered, how their attitudes differ and whether domestic subjects should be taught to both sexes. Using contemporary teaching materials, syllabuses and classroom observations, this informative study provides a detailed picture of home economics in schools now, and questions whether this subject has had its day or not.

READ IT TO ME, NOW!
Learning at Home and at School

Hilary Minns

Read it to me, Now! is a book about five four-year-olds who will all become pupils at the same primary school. It covers both the pre-school period, focussing on the children's backgrounds and their experience of reading and writing, and the first few months of school – their developing awareness of themselves as readers and writers. Hilary Minns points out that children do not arrive at school as 'non-readers', but as having unique reading histories of their own, learnt socially and culturally within their family and community. There is Gemma, from a working-class family, who, at first unused to handling books in the home, slowly changes literacy practices in the family; Gurdeep, arriving at school with a rich knowledge of sacred Sikh tales his mother heard as a girl in India; Anthony, already with a highly developed sense of narrative, learnt mainly from stories and TV dramas; Geeta, who took herself seriously as a reader long before she came to school; and Reid, arriving at school with the feeling that reading was something easily achieved. In drawing together these stories, Hilary Minns illuminatingly suggests ways towards the creation of a total literacy environment for children while recognising the individual character of each child's reading history.

Other Virago Books of Interest:

DEMOCRACY IN THE KITCHEN
Regulating Mothers and Socialising Daughters

Valerie Walkerdine and Helen Lucey

How are daughters raised, how are mothers made to be 'proper' mothers, and what does all this have to do with democracy? From the post-war period, with its emphasis on expanding educational possibilities for all children, to equal opportunities in the 1970s and '80s, the prevailing notion has been that 'natural' mothering (for how could it be otherwise?) would produce 'normal' children, fit for the new democratic age. These ideas have become commonsense ones, but at what cost to the lives of women? Valerie Walkerdine and Helen Lucey explore these effects by examining a well-known study of four-year-olds with their mothers, and in doing so, they tell us a different story about the divides of class and gender and the consequent social inequalities. The authors argue that although ideas from developmental psychology are held to be progressive, they serve to support the view that there is something wrong with working-class mothering which could be put right by making it more middle-class. But nor is the middle-class home one of happy normality: in both classes, women are differently, but oppressively, regulated. In this provocative book, the authors call for a new feminist engagement with class and gender socialisation to constitute a new politics of difference.

THE HEART OF THE RACE

Black Women's Lives in Britain

Beverley Bryan, Stella Dadzie and Suzanne Scafe

Winner of the Martin Luther King Memorial Prize 1985

'A balanced tribute to the undefeated creativity, resilience and resourcefulness of Black women in Britain today' – Margaret Busby, *New Society*

'A long overdue opportunity to set the record straight . . . a considerable achievement' – Brenda Polan, *Guardian*

'Our aim has been to tell it as we know it, placing our story within its history at the heart of our race, and using our own voices and lives to document the day-to-day realities of Afro-Caribbean women in Britain over the past forty years.'

The Heart of the Race powerfully records what life is like for Black women in Britain: grandmothers drawn to the promise of the 'mother country' in the 1950s talk of a different reality; young girls describe how their aspirations at school are largely ignored; working women tell of their commitments to families, jobs, communities. With clarity and determination, these Afro-Caribbean women discuss their treatment by the Welfare State, their housing situations, their health, their self-images – and their confrontation with the racism they encounter all too often. Here too is Black women's celebration of their culture and their struggle to create a new social order in this country.

THE TIDY HOUSE
Little Girls' Writing

Carolyn Steedman

Three working-class eight-year-old girls write a story, 'The Tidy House'. It is about the house they will live in one day, the streets of their own decaying urban estate, about love and motherhood and the pattern of life they expect to inherit. The children in the story are themselves as they believe their parents see them – longed for, yet because of poverty, also sources of irritation and resentment.

In analysing this fascinating document, the author uses her remarkable perceptions of children's writing and their expectations of the world, as well as literature, linguistics, theories of education and history, to come to her highly original and controversial conclusions on how children confront the way things are and imagine the way things might be.

'. . . very interesting and heartening. Seeing the problems and rewards of children's perceptions and writings that close is a great help to understanding a much wider and more persistent process' – *Raymond Williams*

'. . . a revelation – superbly constructed and illuminating. Opens up new ways of looking at the way children learn' – *Dale Spender*